Trials—
DON'T RESENT THEM
AS INTRUDERS
SECOND EDITION

JUANITA PURCELL

REGULAR BAPTIST
RBP Press

DEDICATION

To the ladies in the Ladies' Bible Study at Tri Couny Baptist Church, The Villages, Florida. You graciously allowed me to teach this study to you before it was published.

ACKNOWLEDGEMENT

Poems on pages 13 and 20 are from *Lord, I Keep Running Back to You* by Ruth Harms Calkins. © 1979 Ruth Harms Calkins. Used by permission of Tyndale House Publishers, Inc. All rights reserved.

Trials—Don't Resent Them as Intruders
Second Edition
© 1991, 2009 Regular Baptist Press • Arlington Heights, Illinois
www.RegularBaptistPress.org • 800-727-4440
Printed in U.S.A. All rights reserved.
RBP5395 • ISBN: 978-1-59402-994-3

Fourth printing—2017

Contents

Preface

"Everywhere we turn we find hurting people whose lives are filled with disappointment, despair, and doubt. Yes, life is full of trials. Some have more, some have less, but all have some." I wrote those words in 1991 in the preface of the first Bible study I ever wrote, *Trials—Don't Resent Them as Intruders*.

Nothing has changed in people's lives over the past two decades. Everyone is still having trials! However, I have changed as a result of the trials God has allowed in my life. I have some new insight and answers to the four questions that are considered in this study:

- Why does God allow trials?
- How can we handle trials?
- What can we learn from trials?
- How can we have joy in the midst of trials?

As you find the answers to these questions, you will learn to face your trials head on and not run from them; rather, you will learn from them.

I pray that as you study these lessons you will have a new understanding as to why God allows trials. I trust the things you learn will help you to handle your trials and learn what God wants to teach you through the trial. Most of all, I pray you will learn to have joy in the midst of your trials.

—Juanita Purcell

God's Plan of Salvation

Carefully ponder these Scripture verses, as they explain how you can have a personal relationship with Jesus Christ.

God loves you and wants you to enjoy the abundant life He offers you.

- John 3:16—"For God so loved the world, that he gave his only begotten Son, that whosoever believeth in him should not perish, but have everlasting life."
- John 10:10—Jesus said, "I am come that they might have life, and that they might have it more abundantly."

Man is sinful, and his sin separates him from God.

- Romans 3:23—"For all have sinned, and come short of the glory of God."
- Romans 6:23—"For the wages of sin is death [spiritual separation from God]."

Jesus Christ's death is the only provision God has made to pay for man's sin.

- Romans 5:8—"But God commendeth [demonstrated] his love toward us, in that, while we were yet sinners, Christ died for us."
- John 14:6—"Jesus saith unto him, I am the way, the truth, and the life: no man cometh unto the Father, but by me."

You must receive Jesus Christ as your Savior before you can personally experience His love for you and the abundant life He has planned for you.

- John 1:12—"But as many as received him, to them gave he power to become the sons of God, even to them that believe on his name."

You can invite Christ into your life right now by an act of faith.

- Ephesians 2:8, 9—"For by grace are ye saved through faith; and that not of yourselves: it is the gift of God: not of works, lest any man should boast."

Are you ready to invite Christ into your life to be your Savior? Use the following prayer as a guide to help you express your desire to God: "Lord God, I know I am a sinner and need Your forgiveness. I believe Jesus died for my sins. Right now I receive Him as my Savior. Take control of my life, and replace all the restlessness and anxiety with peace and contentment."

If you have prayed this prayer, tell your Bible study leader or a friend who has been trying to help you.

Learn to trust God's Word—not your feelings—when doubts come.

- Romans 10:13—"For whosoever shall call upon the name of the Lord shall be saved."
- 1 John 5:11–13—"And this is the record, that God hath given to us eternal life, and this life is in his Son. He that hath the Son hath life; and he that hath not the Son of God hath not life. These things have I written unto you that believe on the name of the Son of God; that ye may know that ye have eternal life, and that ye may believe on the name of the Son of God."

Why Trials?
To Make Us More like Jesus

"For whom he did foreknow, he also did predestinate to be conformed to the image of his Son" (Romans 8:29).

Why did their son end up on drugs?
Why did her husband die?
Why did I get cancer?
Why did Daddy lose his job?

Perhaps as you begin this Bible study, you feel like the lady who wrote these words: "I can't believe it. I just barely picked up the pieces of my life and felt like I was coming out of the deep pit I'd been in for so long, and now something has happened to make my pit deeper than it has ever been before. Why, God, again? I feel so weak! Couldn't You wait until I was a little stronger? Couldn't You wait until a little more joy has come into my life? Couldn't You wait, God? Did You forget, God? I am one of Your children, and I love You. Why again?"[1]

Maybe you've asked those same questions. Why? Why? Why? What is the reason Christians hurt so badly? God allows trials in our lives for various reasons.

 1. Read Job 5:7. Why should we not be surprised when trials make a sudden intrusion in our lives?

 2. Look up each of the following references and discover what God says will happen to true disciples.
    Matthew 5:11

John 15:20   *We will be persecuted as Jesus was*

Romans 8:17   *We will suffer but we will also share in His glory.*

2 Timothy 3:12   *We will suffer persecution*

James 1:2, 3   *Our faith will be tested in order patience, endurance*

Isaiah 55:8+9

1 Peter 2:21   *He gave us an example*

Romans 8:28 and 29 contain four truths that can fortify and stabilize God's children *when* trials come. Notice I said *when*, not *if*. "My brethren, count it all joy *when* ye fall into divers [various] temptations" (James 1:2; emphasis added). Let's look at these four truths.

Truth # 1: Go with what you know—not what you feel.

    3. Read Romans 8:28 and 29.

      (a) What are the first three words of verse 28?

            And we know

Romans 5:3+4

      (b) What do "we know" about our trials?

    4. How can we forget what "we know" when our emotions or feelings take over?

We lose our focus on God.

    "Just as we must learn to obey God one choice at a time, we must also learn to trust God one circumstance at a time," says Jerry Bridges. "Trusting God is not a matter of my feelings but of my will. I never feel like trusting God when adversity strikes, but I can choose to do so even when I don't feel like it."[2]

    5. List five things you know about God and His nature from these verses.

      Psalm 34:8   *The Lord is good.*

Psalm 145:17 Righteous + Gracious

Jeremiah 31:3 Loving Kindness; Faithfulness

2 Thessalonians 1:5, 6 God will do the judging

Hebrews 13:5, 6 Will not leave us or forsake us.

6. When trials come, we may tend to doubt the things that we know. Read Isaiah 50:10. What should we do when we seem to be walking in darkness?

7. Read 2 Corinthians 10:3–5. What are we to do with our thoughts?

If we do not bring our thoughts under God's control, then Satan will control them and get a stronghold in our lives. When we dwell on things we can imagine would happen or on negative thoughts that turn our attention away from God, our minds put us in a prison of doubt and fear.

8. How can we replace the negative thoughts? Read Psalm 119:11 and Isaiah 26:3.

We are often tempted to think negatively during what we call "night seasons." "Night seasons are not just a dry time in our lives, but a Father-filtered period of time where God draws us closer to Himself. It's a time where there is no known sin in our lives, and yet God allows circumstances that darken our understanding, that negate our feelings and that put to confusion all our own plans and purposes. It's a time where He lovingly removes all of our natural and comfortable 'support systems' (inside and out) so that He might replace them with total and unshakeable trust in Him."[3]

We *know* God's Word is true, so we must feed our minds on it—especially in times when we are tempted to doubt. I have compiled a list of verses that I call "Why Sink When You Can Swim?" verses (pp. 53, 54). Start memorizing these verses and filling your mind with the positive words of Scripture.

"Sometimes in pain we discount the value of truth by saying, 'But I only know God's truth from the neck up; it doesn't make sense in my heart.' That's OK! It's what you know from the neck up that will enable you to keep your head up. In time, it *will* make sense in your heart. Just don't let go of the truth."[4]

Truth #2: Remember that believers are under construction—not finished products.

> 9. How does Philippians 1:6 illustrate the truth that "believers are always under construction"?

> 10. Someone once illustrated the trial of our faith as a staircase to glory. How could this illustration relate to Romans 8:28 and 29?

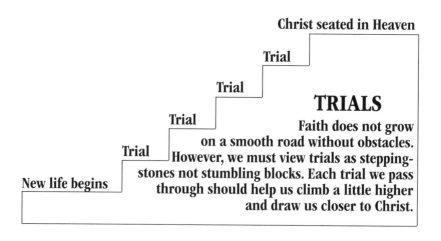

Christ seated in Heaven

Trial

Trial

Trial

Trial

Trial

New life begins

TRIALS

Faith does not grow on a smooth road without obstacles. However, we must view trials as stepping-stones not stumbling blocks. Each trial we pass through should help us climb a little higher and draw us closer to Christ.

11. Romans 8:28 says that "all things work together for good." According to Romans 8:29, is God referring to our material good or our spiritual good?

Seeing what is for our spiritual good is a matter of perspective: "Like street-level parade viewers, we see only one segment of life at a time—a trial now and again, followed by a spiritual refreshing. But God sees the whole parade of life, the beginning and the end and everything in between. . . . Someday, when the parade is over, we will see all of life from His heavenly perspective, and we will exclaim, 'What a great parade! It couldn't have been better!' "[5]

Truth #3: Recognize that Romans 8:28 and 29 are for a select group—not for everyone.

12. Does God say "all things work together for good" for *all* people? To whom is the promise directed?   *To those who love the Lord.*

13. Read John 14:23. What is true of a person who loves God?

Truth #4: Understand God's purpose for us—Christlikeness.

14. What does "called according to his purpose" mean?

As we become like Christ, God causes all things to work together for good. J. C. Brumfield explains: " 'All things work together for good'—not for pleasure, comfort, prosperity, health, or joy, but for good. What is 'the good'? It is the good of the *soul* rather than the *body*; the good of the *eternal* rather than the *present*."[6]

15. How do each of the following passages remind us that God is more concerned with our spiritual growth than with our having comfortable lives?

1 Peter 1:6, 7

Psalm 119:71

Job 23:10

2 Corinthians 12:7–10

16. Trials should produce spiritual growth and cause us to draw closer
to Christ. How do we gain the strength we need for times of trial?
Read Philippians 4:13.

17. What has God been doing in your life to draw you closer to Him?

Let's review the four truths from Romans 8:28 and 29:

Truth #1: Go with what you know—not what you feel.

Truth #2: Remember that believers are under construction—not finished products.

Truth #3: Recognize that Romans 8:28 and 29 are for a select group—
not for everyone.

Truth #4: Understand God's purpose for us—Christlikeness.

FROM MY HEART

You may be studying Romans 8:28 and 29 for the first time. You may
have known Romans 8:28 but never really understood that verse 28 is in-
complete without verse 29.

I remember well when Romans 8:28 and 29 became real in my life. I
had been teaching a ladies' Bible study, and the theme was about becoming more like Jesus. Romans 8:28 and 29 were woven into several lessons.
I began to realize that God allows all the good and all the bad in our lives

for one ultimate purpose: to make us more like Jesus.

We started this lesson with the question, Why does God allow trials? I am learning more and more that trials are custom-made by God to draw us closer to Him and make us more like His Son, Jesus Christ. So the next time I am in the midst of a trial and I began to think, "What good can ever come out of this mess?" I need to remind myself, "The only good I may ever see is that it helps me to grow spiritually and to become more like Jesus." Since that is God's ultimate goal for my life, I made it my number-one goal many years ago. However, time after time I have had to remind myself of that goal so I can stay on course in my journey toward Christlikeness. My heart is saying what Ruth Harms Calkin has written:

Change me, God
Please change me.
Though I cringe
Kick
Resist and resent
Pay no attention to me whatever.
When I run and hide
Drag me out of my safe little shelter.
Change me totally
Whaever it takes
However long You must work at the job.
Change me—and save me
From spiritual self-destruction.[7]

FROM YOUR HEART

Think about this lesson. How did God speak to your heart? What experience stands out in your mind as one God has used for your spiritual growth to draw you closer to Him? Was the pain worth the gain? Why?

Notes

1. Donna Carlson, personal writing (The Villages, FL)—edited for use in this book.

2. Jerry Bridges, "Is God in Control?" *Spirit of Revival* (Buchanan, MI: Life Action Ministries, March 2002), 9.

3. Nancy Missler, *Faith in the Night Seasons—Personal Application Workbook* (Coeur d'Alene, ID: Koinonia House, 2000), 9.

4. Joseph M. Stowell, *Through the Fire* (Wheaton, IL: Victor Books, 1985), 45.

5. James T. Dyet, *How to Handle Life's Hurts* (Schaumburg, IL: Regular Baptist Press, 2005), 33, 34.

6. J. C. Brumfield, *Comfort for Troubled Christians* (Chicago: Moody Press, 1961), 46.

7. Ruth Harms Calkin, *Lord, I Keep Running Back to You* (Wheaton, IL: Tyndale House, 1979), 46.

Why Trials?
To Bring Glory to God

*Therefore I take pleasure in infirmities, in reproaches, in
necessities, in persecutions, in distresses for Christ's sake:
for when I am weak, then I am strong" (2 Corinthians
12:10).*

G od allows trials for several reasons. One of them, as we learned in
lesson 1, is to make His children more like His Son, Jesus Christ
(Romans 8:28, 29). In His sovereignty, God also allows trials to
bring glory to Him.

God's sovereignty is His rulership over all creation.

1. What do the following verses teach about God's sovereignty?

1 Chronicles 29:11, 12

Psalm 115:3

Isaiah 46:9, 10   There is no other.

Daniel 4:17, 34, 35   His plan is to conform us to His
image

Ecclesiastes 7:14

2. Read 1 Corinthians 6:19 and 20 and 10:31 and Colossians 3:17.
   (a) What does it mean to "glorify" someone?

(b) What does it mean to glorify God in our lives?

God often uses trials and tragedies to get our attention and the attention of others as well. When these difficult times come, people around us stop to notice how we will handle our trials. If we handle them God's way, with His strength and power, we bring glory to Him. If we handle them our way, the same way the world would, we will be miserable and bring dishonor to God.

3. When trials come, it is as if we are on center stage; it is our opportunity to be a channel for God's glory. Share a trial you have had in which you were able to display God's greatness and power. Or share a story of someone you know who has used trial and tragedy for God's glory.

"Our trouble becomes the stage of God's triumph. A stage where He can become credible and visible to a world watching with curious eyes. In this context, our pain is a prelude to fulfilling our purpose in life. Pain is a setting in which we can uniquely magnify God."[1]

God uses triumph as well as trials to make Himself visible in our lives. Review the account of the blind man in John 9.

4. According to verse 3, what was Christ's ultimate purpose for this man's life?

5. What did Jesus do for the blind man (vv. 6–11)?

God uses both tragedy and triumph in our lives so that we might be a reflection of His glory in this dark world that needs to know our God is real and powerful.

6. Tell of a triumph in your life that God used to glorify Himself.

Joni Eareckson Tada is a beautiful example of a person who brought glory to God through her tragedy. Joni became a quadriplegic as a result of a diving accident when she was a teenager. She wrote the following words nine years after her accident: "We aren't always responsible for the circumstances in which we find ourselves. However, we are responsible for the way we respond to them. . . . I saw that my injury was not a tragedy but a gift God was using to help me conform to the image of Christ, something that would mean my ultimate satisfaction, happiness—even joy."[2]

— How important is it to God that His glory be displayed in our lives? It's so important to Him that He will interrupt our health and happiness in order for His purpose to be accomplished.

7. Read 2 Corinthians 12:7–10. What was the purpose for Paul's trial?

8. Paul did not have a thorn because he had sinned but to keep him from sin. God arranged a plan to keep Paul's pride in check. Paul's pride could have destroyed him. What was Paul's reaction to his trial (2 Corinthians 12:9)?

9. God refused to relieve Paul's burden, so Paul made a new discovery in his life of faith. What did he discover (2 Corinthians 12:9, 10)? God's grace is sufficient

10. How could Paul's weakness be an opportunity for God to be glorified in his life?

Vance Havner put it succinctly, "Lord, You have the strength and I have the weakness—let's team up!"[3]

11. Read Romans 4:16–21.

    (a) How did Abraham give glory to God?

    (b) What was the promise (Genesis 17:15–19)?

    (c) Why do you think God waited until Abraham was one hundred years old to fulfill the promise?

12. Read Luke 17:11–16. How did the Samaritan who was healed of his leprosy glorify God?

13. Why should we be willing to give public praise to God when He demonstrates His mercy in our lives? (See Psalms 34:1–3; 40:3; 107:2.)

Proverbs 24:10

Kay Arthur explains how this works: "As you so well know, most of the world around you doesn't read the Bible. So what does God do? God shows the world pictures of Himself and of the sufficiency of His grace through your life. . . . In any of a variety of disappointments, He lets you hurt as others hurt, knowing that the way in which you handle this hurt will be an undeniable testimony that there's something awesomely different about you."[4]

14. It may seem hard to walk with God when things don't work out the way we had planned, or when our world comes tumbling down and loved ones and friends can't help. Why do some people faint in the day of adversity? Read Proverbs 24:10.

15. When our strength is small, how can we increase it? Read Isaiah
    40:31.

"We have a purpose, a divine destiny. Our purpose is to glorify God
through our lives. If God should select you to bring glory to Him in this
world through pain, do it well. Obey. Bear witness. Through your suffering,
some may seek and find the Saviour. Let them hear you sing: To God be the
glory, / Great things He hath done!"[5]

16. How did Job's testing reveal God's glory? Read Job 1:1–22; 13:15;
    19:25, 26; 23:10.

17. Read Job 42:2. What did Job acknowledge about God that allowed
    him to praise Him when his trials were over?
    God can do everything

Fanny Crosby became blind at the age of six weeks as a result of a doctor's blunder. At the age of eight she wrote:

O what a happy soul am I
Although I cannot see,
I am resolved that in this world
Contented I will be.

How many blessings I enjoy
That other people don't!
So weep and sigh because I'm blind,
I cannot, and I won't!

18. Look in a hymnbook for songs written by Fanny Crosby. How was
    God glorified in her life?

Why does God allow trials in our lives? For our growth and His glory. Have you ever considered that your trial is an opportunity for God to display His glory in your life? Does that give you a new perspective on your trial?

FROM MY HEART

When I think of people whose trials have brought glory to God, my first thoughts go to people like Amy Carmichael, Jim and Elisabeth Elliot, Joni Eareckson Tada, Corrie Ten Boom, and the list could go on and on. But what about all those whom we have never heard about? those who faithfully endured years of trials without complaining or running from them? Their focus in life was not on comfort but Christlikeness, and, as a result, their lives brought glory to God.

As I look back over the last several years of my life, I see periods of difficult trials. As I was passing through them, I often wondered why. I realize now that God wanted to use those trials for His glory. My writing ministry has been enriched because of the trials God has allowed in my life.

I did not write the following words, but they express what my heart is feeling.

God, I am destined for You!
I was created for You!
Nothing I can ever do or think or feel
Can be separated from You.
With all my inner struggles
My self-absorption
My lethargy and fraud
I cannot alter to one degree
Your settled intention
Your divine purpose:
I was made to bring glory to You![6]

FROM YOUR HEART

Review this lesson. How did God speak to your heart? Have you ever considered that the purpose of your trial could be that God's glory would be visible in your life? If so, in what way?

Notes

1. Stowell, *Through the Fire*, 114.

2. Joni Eareckson, *Joni* (Grand Rapids: Zondervan Publishing House, 1976), 154.

3. Vance Havner, *Though I Walk through the Valley* (Old Tappan, NJ: Fleming H. Revell, 1974), 20.

4. Kay Arthur, *As Silver Refined* (Colorado Springs: Waterbrook Press, 1997), 41.

5. Stowell, 120.

6. Calkins, 26.

Why Trials?
To Correct Us

"Now no chastening for the present seemeth to be joyous,
but grievous: nevertheless afterward it yieldeth the peace-
able fruit of righteousness unto them which are exercised
thereby" (Hebrews 12:11).

God's ultimate goal for us is to be conformed to the image of His Son, Jesus Christ. If we refuse to go along with God's plan for our lives, He will just keep turning up the heat until we are no longer comfortable. In fact, He may have to make us absolutely miserable before we say, "Okay, Lord, I'm tired of fighting You. I surrender; You win."

   1. Read Proverbs 13:24; 19:18; 22:15; 23:13; 29:15–17. What do these verses teach about wise, loving parents?

   2. How does our wise, loving Heavenly Father deal with His children? Read Hebrews 12:5 and 6.

"Chasten" is an old word that carries the idea of "punishment." But the Greek word that is translated "chasten" primarily means "to train children." Today we would probably use the word "discipline."

No matter how old we are, God sees us as His children who still need His training and discipline. He never stops teaching us how to be more like Jesus.

I never realized discipline was an act of love until we had our first child. This made God's discipline more understandable to me. A parent's discipline, if given in love, will develop respect and deepen his or her relationship with the child. In our relationship with our Heavenly Father, Who always disciplines in love, the same should be true.

    3. In some people's minds, love and pain cannot go hand and hand. How would Hebrews 12:6 refute this thinking?

    4. If parents do not discipline their children, what message are they giving their children according to Proverbs 13:24?

    5. When parents discipline their child, they may explain that it is for the child's good. What does God say about His discipline? Read Hebrews 12:9 and 10.

    6. What does God want His chastening to accomplish in His child's life? Read Hebrews 12:9–11.

    7. What word in Hebrews 12:6 indicates that God's discipline is often severe?

Scourging, or flogging, was a very severe form of punishment in Bible times. It was a beating with a whip that had leather straps on it. Broken glass or pieces of bone or metal were tied at the end of each strap. The Lord Jesus was scourged before He was crucified (Matthew 27:26). Scourging was a horrible beating, often administered in conjunction with capital punishment.

    8. Since the Scriptures use the word "scourge" in relation to God's disciplining us, what does that suggest about His discipline?

Charles Stanley asks, "How far is God willing to go? How much pain dare He inflict?" Then he answers, "I think . . . that God will do whatever it takes. As much as He must hate pain, He hates sin that much worse. As much as He must despise suffering, He loves us that much more."[1]

9. How can we discern if our trial is a testing of our faith or a disciplinary measure from God? Read Psalms 19:12–14 and 139:23 and 24. Also see James 1:2–4.

10. Read James 1:14 and 15. If God allows us to continue in our sinful ways, what is the eventual outcome?

Pastor Stanley goes on to say: "God's goal in discipline is not simply to make us behave. His purpose is to make us holy, to bring us into conformity with His Son. . . . Through this process, our character will be fine-tuned to reflect the character of Christ Himself. Because God knows us inside and out, He can tailor our discipline in such a way to accomplish just that."[2]

11. If a professing believer continues in sin year after year without God's chastening, what might we conclude? Read Hebrews 12:7 and 8 and 1 John 2:19.

God is patient and long-suffering with His children. Sometimes it seems our sin goes unnoticed, but it isn't! God loves us too much to let us continue in our sin. "For whom the Lord loveth he chasteneth" (Hebrews 12:6).

God is merciful. He forgives us and delivers us out of our troubles when we confess our sin (1 John 1:9). "Who is a God like unto thee, that pardoneth iniquity, and passeth by the transgression of the remnant of his heritage? He retaineth not his anger for ever, because he delighteth in mercy" (Micah 7:18).

Jonah is a good example of God's discipline of one of His children.

12. Read Jonah 1:3. Why did God bring a storm of correction into Jonah's life?

13. Read Jonah 1:4 and 17. An old gospel song says, "With God things don't just happen; every step by Him is planned." How was this true in Jonah's life?

14. Read Jonah 2:7. What did Jonah do when he was in trouble?

15. Read Jonah 2:7—3:3. What did God want His correction to produce in Jonah's life?

16. God delivers us after we have learned our lesson. According to Jonah 1:17, how many days did Jonah need to learn his lesson?

17. A deed once done cannot be undone. What does Galatians 6:7 mean when it says we reap what we sow?

18. Lessons should never be wasted. What is a lesson you have learned in days of testing and correction?

One writer has observed that "no matter how far away from God you've gone, when you surrender your life to the Lord, a path is carved from where you are to where you are supposed to be, and He puts you on it. . . . As you take one step at a time, holding God's hand and letting Him lead, He will get you where you need to go."[3]

FROM MY HEART

As I look back over my life as a young mother of three sons, I think one of the hardest parts of my job was knowing when and how to discipline the boys. My husband and I took God's Word literally when it says, "Withhold not correction from the child: for if thou beatest him with the rod, he shall not die" (Proverbs 23:13). I remember how I hated to spank my sons, but I knew I had to break their stubborn will so they could learn to obey me and God.

As they grew older and serious issues required more severe discipline, their father took care of those situations. Hebrews 12:9 says, "We have had fathers of our flesh which corrected us, and we gave them reverence." I believe a child's reverence and respect for his or her parents springs from proper discipline. We are blessed to have three sons who honor and respect us and God. One of the reasons we enjoy this blessing is because we took time to discipline them—God's way.

I hate to think what their lives would be like if we had given up on our discipline. I would also hate to think what my life would be like today if God had not disciplined my stubborn, rebellious will. I wanted my way, no matter what. Praise the Lord, He didn't give up on me, and He still works on me when I start to get out of line.

FROM YOUR HEART

What did you learn from this lesson about God's discipline? Are you in the midst of a trial right now? If so, how do you know if your trial is a testing of your faith or a discipline from God? If you know God is disciplining you because of known sin in your life, what are you going to do about it?

Notes

1. Charles Stanley, *How to Handle Adversity* (Nashville: Thomas Nelson Publishers, 1989), 93.

2. Ibid., 96.

3. Stormie Omartian, *Just Enough Light for the Step I'm On* (Eugene, OR: Harvest House Publishers, 1999), 13, 14.

L E S S O N 4

Don't Run from Trials— Learn from Them

"My brethren, count it all joy when ye fall into divers [various] temptations [trials]. Knowing this, that the trying of your faith worketh patience. But let patience have her perfect work, that ye may be perfect and entire, wanting nothing" (James 1:2–4).

Another translation of James 1:2 says we shouldn't look at trials as intruders and resent them, but are to welcome them as friends. It's a big order to "count it all joy" when trials come and to welcome them as friends and not intruders. This seems like an unreasonable command. But it's not! God never gives a command without a reason.

When we view this as an unreasonable command, we miss the point: "All too often trials prompt groanings and complaints. . . . Trials are not to be seen as tribulations but testings. . . . James gave sound advice on how to score high on every test. One who brings the right attitude to the trial, who understands the advantage of the trial, and who knows where to obtain assistance in the trial will certainly end up on God's honor roll."[1]

Let's take James 1:2–4 apart and see how we can view trials as advantages rather than intruders.

We must have the right attitude about trials (James 1:2).

1. Read James 1:2 and Isaiah 43:2. What word in these two verses indicates trials should not surprise us or seem an intrusion into our lives when they come?

So, *when* the trials come, " 'count it all joy when you fall into various trials.' Don't rebel! Don't faint! Rejoice! These problems are not enemies, bent on destroying you. They are friends which have come to aid you to develop Christian character."[2]

The word "count" means "consider." Knowing trials will come, we need to consider the value of trials before they come.

2. When a trial makes a sudden intrusion into our lives, we may not feel joyful. However, what does Isaiah 26:3 tell us we can experience?

3. If we consider the benefit of trials before they come, how can we respond in the midst of them? Read Romans 8:28 and 29.

"Most of us still rate the events of our lives as either a 'good' thing or a 'bad' thing, but when we're finally able to merge all the events of our lives into the category of a God thing, then we will be where He wants us."[3]

4. If we don't consider the benefit of trials before they come, how might we respond in the midst of the trials? Read Hebrews 12:15.

5. How could facing a trial be compared to facing surgery or taking medicine?

John the Baptist, the one who proclaimed the coming of Christ, was in prison. As he contemplated his plight, he began to wonder if Jesus really is Who He said He is. "Art thou he that should come, or do we look for another?" (Matthew 11:4). John was struggling with the trial he was experiencing.

So Jesus told John's disciples to report to John some of His miracles, and then He added these words: "Blessed is he, whosoever shall not be offended in me" (Matthew 11:6). The blessing comes to the one who does not "stumble" over Jesus.

    6. In what ways might our trials cause us to "stumble" over Jesus/ God?

    7. What is the state of mind—and being—of those who don't stumble over what God is doing in their lives (Matthew 11:6)?

To not stumble but to be blessed, we must have faith—tested faith: "Faith must be tested, because it can only become your intimate possession through conflict. What is challenging your faith right now? The test will either prove your faith right, or it will kill it. Jesus said, 'Blessed is he who is not offended because of Me' (Matthew 11:6). . . . Faith is absolute trust in God—trust that could never imagine that He would forsake us (see Hebrews 13:5–6)."[4]

In order to handle our trials, we must have the right attitude about trials. James 1:3 and 4 give a second principle.

We must understand the advantage of the trial (James 1:3, 4).

The words "temptations" (trials) in verse 2 and "trying" (testing) in verse 3 carry basically the same meaning. They both give the idea of testing something to prove its genuineness. "Patience" in verse 3 is often translated "endurance," an inner strength that continually increases under testing.

    8. In light of these word meanings, write verse 3 in your own words.

    9. How might we short-circuit the development of endurance in our lives?

10. James 1:12 names the reward for enduring trials. What is it?

"The term for 'crown' is borrowed from athletics rather than royalty. It was a wreath placed on the victor's head in athletic events, symbolizing persevering triumph. And a more literal translation could be 'the crown which is life,' that is, eternal life. Consequently, a more accurate statement of the principle is this: perseverance attests to God's approval, for it gives evidence of eternal life (salvation)."[5]

The word "perfect" in verse 4 does not refer to sinless perfection; it means spiritual maturity. God wants us to be mature, well-rounded believers who are not lacking in any of the spiritual graces of the Spirit pictured in Galatians 5:22 and 23: love, joy, peace, longsuffering, gentleness (kindness), goodness, faith (faithfulness), meekness, and temperance (self-control).

11. Read 1 Peter 5:10.

    (a) What four words did Peter use to describe what happens after we have "suffered a while"?

    (b) Use synonyms of Peter's words to describe what trials do for your faith.

"Christians are to live with the understanding that God's purposes realized in the future require some pain in the present. While the believer is being personally attacked by the enemy, he is being personally perfected by the Lord, as the next phrase attests. . . . perfect, establish, strengthen, and settle. These 4 words [perfect, establish, strengthen, settle] all speak of strength and resoluteness. God is working through the Christian's struggles to produce strength of character."[6]

James 1:3 starts with "knowing this." What have we learned about trials in verses 2–4?

- We know trials will come. God says, "when," not "if."
- We know trials will vary in length and intensity.
- We know trials prove the quality of our faith.
- We know we are to endure trials, not run from them.
- We know trials help us grow spiritually.

One thing we may not know is how to handle our trials. That's why God says, "If any of you lack wisdom" (James 1:5).

We must know where to get help in times of trial (James 1:5).

12. When trials make a sudden intrusion into our lives, what are we often prone to do before we ask for God's wisdom?

13. Read James 1:5 and 3:17. How would you describe the kind of wisdom James presents?

14. Read James 1:6–8.Why is it so easy to forget what we *know* when we are in the midst of a trial?

15. How can applying Proverbs 3:5 and 6 to our lives correct double-mindedness?

16. Read James 1:5 again. What assurance do you have from this verse that God wants us to come to Him for wisdom?

"The Bible does not give specific answers to the innumerable problems that arise in life. It does not solve problems in so many words, but God's word does give general principles. We must apply these principles to problems as they arise day by day. That is why we need wisdom. Spiritual wisdom is the practical application of our Lord's teachings to everyday situations."[7]

17. Why is it often easier to reach for a cell phone than our heavenly prayer line when a trial invades our lives?

Sometimes we ask for God's wisdom, and God doesn't say yes, no, go, stay, wait. He is just silent! When we can't hear anything, we must remember He may be trying to quietly whisper in our ear, "Endure!"

18. Read Romans 5:3 and 4. How is endurance developed?

"We mustn't pray for relief from the trial, but rather pray for strength to endure it with courage, humility and love, and be changed by it. We won't be able to weather the storms unless we are willing to persevere and overcome. Romans 5:3 tells us that tribulation brings patience, and patience, if we allow it, will bring about hope."[8]

FROM MY HEART

James 1:2–4 seems to have some shocking truths about trials. The thought of pain and suffering as part of the process of growing spiritually seems unlikely. Yet God's Word stands!

The first time I realized that James was talking about welcoming trials as friends rather than resenting them as intruders, I thought, "No way!" Now—some twenty years later—I realize it works! Every time I head into another trial, I say to myself, "Juanita, it's time for your faith to be stretched a little more; it's growing time." Then I am faced with a choice: welcome the trial and get better, or resent the trial and get bitter.

The bottom line is a choice between these two:
• Comfortable life
• Conformity to Christ

When I remember that truth, I can learn from my trials rather than run from them. "Lord, I don't always do it, but I'm still trying."

FROM YOUR HEART

How did God speak to your heart in this lesson? What one truth stands out most in your mind? How have you handled trials in the past? Do you usually try to run away from them? Or do you plod through them and endure, no matter what? What needs to change in your life for you to see trials as friends to aid you in developing Christian character?

Notes

1. John Walvoord and Roy B. Zuck, eds., *The Bible Knowledge Commentary: New Testament Edition* (Wheaton, IL: Victor Books, 1983), 820.

2. William MacDonald, *Believer's Bible Commentary* (Nashville: Thomas Nelson Publishers, 1995), 2218.

3. Chuck and Nancy Missler, *Faith in the Night Seasons* (Coeur d' Alene, ID: The King's High Way Ministries, 1999), 67.

4. Oswald Chambers, *My Utmost for His Highest: Updated Edition* (Nashville: Discovery House, 1992), August 29.

5. John MacArthur Jr., *The MacArthur New Testament Commentary: James* (Chicago: Moody Press, 1998), 42.

6. John MacArthur, ed., *The MacArthur Study Bible* (Nashville: Word Publishing, 1997), 1949.

7. MacDonald, 2219.

8. Missler, 169.

L   E   S   S   O   N   5

Have an Attitude of Gratitude

"In every thing give thanks; for this is the will of God in Christ concerning you" (1 Thessalonians 5:18).

"Giving thanks always for all things" (Ephesians 5:20).

If you are like me, it is easy to thank the Lord for all His blessings . . . but thank Him for trials? WOW! "In every thing give thanks" and "giving thanks always" seem like impossible commands to obey. We learned in lesson 1 that God allows trials for our spiritual good (Romans 8:28, 29). God is so concerned about our spiritual growth that He won't just let us glide along on a smooth path too long. He allows the bumps in the road (the trials) to draw us closer to Him. When we realize He loves us enough to give us special attention, we can say, "Thank You, Lord."

1. What do these two verses mean to you? Write your meaning beside each verse.

1 Thessalonians 5:18

Ephesians 5:20

2. What is the difference between 1 Thessalonians 5:18 and Ephesians 5:20?

3. (a) When are we most likely to say, "God is so good"?

(b) Read 1 Peter 1:6 and 7. When are we least likely to say this?

4. Why should we be able to say, "God is so good" all the time? Read Lamentations 3:22–26.

My first reaction to a trial is not usually, "Thank You for this trial, Lord." I certainly couldn't say that I have an attitude of gratitude. My first reaction is usually disappointment. No doubt you might have a similar reaction.

5. How would you define disappointment?

6. Most of us have read these words: "Our disappointments are His appointments." What does that statement mean? Read Psalm 37:23.

If we will, by faith, change the D of disappointment to an H, and add a space, we will see that our disappointment is an ordered appointment from God.

DISAPPOINTMENT—HIS APPOINTMENT

7. How can seeing our disappointments as God's appointments help us thank God for them? Read Jeremiah 29:11.

Another word for gratitude is "thankfulness." "Thanksgiving has great curative power. The heart that is constantly overflowing with gratitude will be safe from those attacks of resentfulness and gloom that bother so many religious persons."[1]

8. If our trials go on and on and we don't see our disappointments as God's appointments, we're headed on a downward spiral. What is the next downward step? Read about the experience of the Israelites in Numbers 21:4 and 5.

9. What is your definition of discouragement?

Discouragement could easily be defined as "without courage." When we are discouraged, thoughts of quitting invade our minds. I often rehearse this thought, "I can't feel discouraged unless I am thinking discouraging thoughts." My attitude definitely determines my altitude—how high or how low I will feel. An attitude of gratitude is so important. I must start giving thanks when discouraging thoughts whirl around in my mind.

The Israelites are a good example of discouraged people. When they were on the verge of entering Canaan, they were not allowed to go in. They wandered in the wilderness for forty years until all the population over twenty years of age had died. A new generation of Israelites was finally ready to enter the Promised Land.

10. Read Deuteronomy 1:21–32. What had caused the Israelites to be discouraged in the first place?

Satan is pleased when we disbelieve God and His promises. A discouraged believer is not an effective believer.

11. How can we ward off Satan's attacks on our minds? Read Ephesians 6:17 and 18 and 2 Corinthians 10:3–5.

12. God says, "In every thing give thanks" (1 Thessalonians 5:18) and "giving thanks always in all things" (Ephesians 5:20). What is the opposite of being thankful?

13. How does Luke 17:12–19 illustrate that people don't automatically have an attitude of thankfulness when God blesses them in a special way?

14. How could we ever be strong enough to thank God for everything He allows in our lives? Read Philippians 4:13, Colossians 1:11, and Romans 8:11.

"To the children of God, everything comes directly from the Father's hand. . . . It may be the sin of man that originates the action, and therefore the thing itself cannot be said to be the will of God; but by the time it reaches us it has become God's will for us, and must be accepted as directly from His hands."[2]

15. God knows it is hard to thank Him when we don't feel thankful. Is it hypocritical to thank Him when we don't feel thankful? Read James 4:17.

16. What are some things you do each day that you don't feel like doing?

17. Read Psalm 107:8, 15, 21, and 31.
    (a) What do these verses suggest about giving thanks?

    (b) For what are we to choose to give thanks?

18. What good things happen in your life each day for which you can give thanks?

Nancy Leigh DeMoss has written: "A grateful spirit is what enables people to view and respond to the most painful circumstances in life with thanksgiving. As one person observed, 'Some people complain because God put thorns on roses, while others praise Him for putting roses among thorns.' "[3]

19. What's happening in your life right now for which you are having a hard time thanking God?

If you are in the midst of a trial and are having a hard time finding anything for which to be thankful, try thanking God for the testing itself and for what it will accomplish in your life.

"But he knoweth the way that I take: when he hath tried me, I shall come forth as gold" (Job 23:10).

Matilda Nordtvedt encourages us that, "yes, there is a 'glory side' to every problem, affliction, perplexity, misunderstanding and loss. It is God's point of view. When we look at things the way He does, our suffering becomes a servant, our trials become treasures, our loss becomes gain, and our pain becomes blessing."[4]

FROM MY HEART

Thanking God for my trials may never become an automatic response. However, I have learned to say more quickly, "Where is God in this?" When I remember that God is in control and nothing can touch my life that God does not allow, it keeps my eyes upward. I recently ran across a term I just love: "Father-filtered." The author's emphasis was that every trial is "Father-filtered"; it passes through God's loving hand before it touches me.

Looking back over my trials, I thank the Lord for many things. Here are three of them:

- I have learned to trust God in ways I had never experienced before. He has taught me what "naked faith" is all about—faith that is not dependent on anything or anyone but God alone.
- I have learned to love my Bible more. It has been a life preserver that has kept me afloat in the stormy trials.
- I have learned to love Heaven more. I can hardly wait to bow at Jesus' feet and thank Him for His faithfulness to me. When I feel I cannot handle another thing, He gives me the strength to go on. When I am faithless, He is faithful. He has never failed me. Praise His holy name!

FROM YOUR HEART

Think carefully about this lesson. How can giving thanks help stabilize your faith in the midst of the storm? Reread the Matilda Nordtvedt quotation on page 38. Write what each one of these statements means to you:

"Suffering becomes a servant"

"Trials become treasures"

"Loss becomes gain"

"Pain becomes blessing"

Ask God to make these truths your own cause for thanksgiving in the hard times of life.

Notes

1. A. W. Tozer. Quoted by Nancy Leigh DeMoss, *The Attitude of Gratitude* (Buchanan, MI: Revive Our Hearts, 1999), 14.

2. Hannah Whitall Smith, *The Christian's Secret of a Happy Life* (Westwood, NJ: Fleming H. Revell Co., 1870), 144.

3. DeMoss, 15.

4. Matilda Nordtvedt, *Living beyond Depression* (Minneapolis: Bethany House Publishers, 1978), 37.

Live a Palms-up Life

"I am crucified with Christ: nevertheless I live; yet not I,
but Christ liveth in me: and the life which I now live in the
flesh I live by the faith of the Son of God, who loved me, and
gave himself for me" (Galatians 2:20).

Most of you who are studying this lesson have probably come to that initial point of surrender that John 3:3 identifies as being "born again." You have recognized that you are a sinner and that only Jesus Christ can save you from sin's penalty, which is death (Romans 6:23). If you have not made this initial decision, please talk to your Bible study leader. She will show you from God's Word how you can become a child of God (John 1:12).

For those of you who are His children, that point of surrender at salvation was just the beginning of a daily life of surrender that says no to self and yes to God. Palms-up living has helped me to do this as I daily surrender my will to do God's will.

Palms-up Living

   1. (a) If someone asked you to surrender, in what position would your hands be?

   (b) So what do you think it means to live a palms-up life?

Years ago I read a statement by Amy Carmichael that helped me so much. It was just four words, but they were—and still are—powerful in my life. She said, "In acceptance lieth peace." God is going to give or take what He wants in our lives. He either does it with us kicking and screaming, or He does it with us evidencing peace and saying, "Whatever, Lord! Give what You want or take what You want." Learning to handle your trials with a spirit of acceptance will help you get better instead of bitter as you move through your trial.

2. How could palms-up living help you handle a trial?

"Open hands should characterize the soul's attitude toward God— open to receive what He wants to give, open to give back what He wants to take. Acceptance of the will of God means relinquishment of our own. If our hands are full of our own plans, there isn't room to receive His."[1]

3. Read Galatians 2:20 and Philippians 4:13. What supernatural power do we have in us, after we are born again, to help us live a crucified, surrendered life? (See also Ephesians 1:19 and 20 and Romans 8:11.)

4. Read Luke 9:23. What three acts make up surrender according to this verse?

-

-

-

"One of the challenges of complete surrender to Christ is that we don't know what lies ahead. . . . We want to see all the fine print so we can read it over, think about it, and then decide whether to sign our name on the dotted line. But that's not God's way. God says instead, 'Here's a blank piece of paper. I want you to sign your name on the bottom line, hand it back to Me, and let Me fill in the details.' . . . If we will let Him, God will fill in the details of our lives with His incomparable wisdom and sovereign plan, written in the indelible ink of His covenant faithfulness and love."[2]

5. In light of Christ's sacrifice for us on the cross, what are we exhorted to offer as a sacrifice? Read Romans 12:1.

6. Old Testament offerings were to be totally consumed on the altar. How is our offering to be different (Romans 12:1)?

I have this thought written in my Bible by Romans 12:1: "Because a living sacrifice can crawl off the altar, we must die daily." Each day I must die to my will so I can be willing to do to God's will.

Palms-up living is a picture of daily presenting ourselves as living sacrifices, saying, "Give what You want; take what You want."

7. Presenting our bodies as living sacrifices is a *reasonable* service according to Romans 12:1. In light of Hebrews 9:14 and 10:5–7, why is palms-up living a *reasonable* sacrifice?

8. Read Jesus' words in Luke 14:25–33. What does Christ ask us to surrender?

9. Luke 14:26 seems to be the ultimate in surrender. Read 1 John 4:20. What do you think Jesus meant?

"And whosoever doth not bear his cross, and come after me, cannot be my disciple" (Luke 14:27).

"Everyone listening to Jesus knew that a cross meant only one thing—death. He was calling them to come and die to everything that competed with His reign and rule in their lives."[3]

Biblical Examples

Daniel was a only a young man when he was taken captive from his home in Israel to Babylon. Even though he was being trained in royal ways, he had purposed not to defile himself (Daniel 1:8). Over the years Daniel rose to second in command in Babylon. But he never lost his heart for God. He continued his practice of praying three times a day—even after the king gave a decree that all people were to pray only to him.

10. What did Daniel's total surrender to God cost him? Read Daniel 6:16.

11. How did God honor Daniel's obedience? Read "the rest of the story" in Daniel 6:22 and 23.

12. Daniel's three friends—Shadrach, Meshach and Abednego—had the same convictions as Daniel. They refused to bow to King Nebuchadnezzar. What did their obedience to God cost them? Read Daniel 3:16–20.

13. How did God honor their obedience? Read Daniel 3:25–28.

14. How did all four of these men display a palms-up life?

Does God always deliver us out of our trials because we are totally committed to do His will? No! Sometimes He thinks it is best for us to endure the trial. Palms-up living can be a bit scary, but God never asks more from us than He gives us the strength to bear. First Corinthians 10:13 talks about our trials, and we are reminded that "God is faithful, who will not suffer you to be tempted [tested] above that ye are able; but will with the temptation [test] also make a way to escape, that ye may be able to bear it."

Betty Stam, a missionary martyr in China, wrote: "Lord, I give up all my plans and purposes, all my own desires and hopes, and accept Thy will for my life. I give myself, my life, my all utterly to Thee to be Thine forever.

Fill me and seal me with Thy Holy Spirit. Use me as Thou wilt, send me where Thou wilt, work out Thy whole will in my life at any cost, now and forever."[4]

Another example of Biblical surrender is Mary, the mother of Jesus.

15. Read Luke 1:26–38. What words indicate Mary's desire to live a palms-up life?

16. What could Mary's surrender have cost her?

17. Has commitment to Christ ever cost you anything? If so, what?

18. The cost is great, but so is the reward. According to Matthew 25:23 what is the reward?

"But precisely what is the cost of commitment? Time, money, promotion, reputation, energy, emotional stamina, or health—all could be part of the cost. God deals with us individually. What is to one person a great price may be a pittance to another. The cost is great. But so is the reward—namely, the true joy of the Christian life when we hear the words (paraphrased by Jerry White), 'Well done, good and faithful slave; you were faithful with a few things, I will put you in charge of many things, enter into the joy of your master.' "[5]

Living a palms-up life is turning loose of everything and trusting God completely. Will we do it willingly, or will God have to pry our fingers open?

FROM MY HEART

I have been practicing palms-up living for about twenty years now. God has patiently tried to teach me to trust Him. I vividly remember when I first started living a palms-up life; and, I have to be honest, it was scary. I was so afraid of what God might take or give that I had a hard time keeping my palms up and open. I often found myself with my fists clenched, and then God would pry my fingers open one by one. However, over the years I have finally learned to keep my palms up and open. The thing that has helped me the most is to daily place everything and every person at the feet of Jesus. When I am able to do that, I no longer fear what God might take from me; I have already given it all to Him. If He sends something I don't want to receive, I don't have to be fearful. I have also learned His grace is sufficient (2 Corinthians 12:9) and He will give me the strength I need to handle the trial (Philippians 4:13).

Palms-up living has changed my life and is teaching me "in whatsoever state I am, therewith to be content"—even trials (Philippians 4:11).

FROM YOUR HEART

Have you been afraid of the word "surrender"? Did this lesson help relieve some of your fears? What have you learned about palms-up living? I would challenge you to try it for thirty days—it could change your life!

Notes

1. Elisabeth Elliot, *A Path through Suffering* (Ann Arbor, MI: Servant Publications, 1990), 69.

2. Nancy Leigh DeMoss, *Surrender* (Chicago: Moody Publishers, 2003), 59, 60.

3. DeMoss, 130.

4. Betty Stam. Quoted by Cynthia Heald, *Becoming a Woman of Excellence* (Colorado Springs, Navpress, 1986), 110.

5. Jerry White, *The Power of Commitment* (Colorado Springs, Navpress, 1985), 51.

Build an Ark of Faith

"But they that wait upon the LORD shall renew their strength;
they shall mount up with wings as eagles; they shall run,
and not be weary; and they shall walk, and not faint"
(Isaiah 40:31).

How can we handle our trials and keep our heads above water when the storm is fierce? I learned many years ago to build an ark of faith. I remember the day I was challenged to do this. I heard these words in a message: "I'm Noah, and you're Noah, and God is calling down from Heaven, 'Noah, build your ark of faith. The sun's shining in your life today. There's no tragedy yet; but Noah, there's a great flood coming. While there's still time, build your ark of faith so when the flood comes, you stay on top of the flood not under it.' " Soon after that I started building my ark of faith.

1. What do you think I mean by "build an ark of faith"?

Protection in times of trouble

Through the years I have compiled a list of Scripture verses. I have memorized them and passed them on to others to memorize. I call them my "Why Sink When You Can Swim?" verses. I keep a list of them in the front of my Bible. These verses have helped strengthen my faith and fortify my soul for the stormy seasons. When I started compiling this list of verses, I didn't know God was preparing me for a long series of trials. The verses were like life preservers to keep my head above water. The verses are listed on pages 53 and 54.

2. What are some of the verses you turn to during difficult days?

The verses we will study in this lesson are included on my list of "Why Sink When You Can Swim" verses. Read the verse or verses before you answer the related questions.

3. Psalm 37:23; Proverbs 3:5 and 6. How does this statement "Make no footprints of your own" relate to these verses?

Let God lead me.

" 'The stops of a good man, as well as his steps, are ordered by the Lord,' says George Müller. . . . I shall never be able to go too fast, if the Lord is in front of me; and I can never go too slowly, if I follow Him always, everywhere. . . . He has left footprints for us to follow. Make no footprints of thine own!"[1]

4. Isaiah 40:31. Someone described Isaiah 40:31 as learning to live the wing-life.

(a) What lesson does having "wings as eagles" suggest?

Strength

(b) The word "renew" means "change, or exchange." How can we exchange our strength for God's strength?

Surrendering to the Lord

(c) What does "wait upon the LORD" mean? (See also Psalm 27:14; 37:7; 62:1, 5; Lamentations 3:25, 26.)

be Patient

5. Psalm 31:15. How does knowing all our circumstances are under God's control keep our faith steady regardless of what happens?

We know God is in control

I often share with ladies that I am in the palm of Christ's hand (John 10:28, 29). God's hand is over Christ's hand, and nothing touches me unless God opens His fingers to allow it. If He does allow a difficult experience, I know it has passed through God's loving hand before it touches me. Everything that touches our lives is "Father-filtered." I love that thought! *Protection through Jesus + God*

 6. <u>Philippians 4:4</u>. We are not told to rejoice in our circumstances but to rejoice in the <u>Lord</u> of our circumstances. What do we know about the Lord from the following Scriptures that could cause us to rejoice no matter what is happening?

Jeremiah 31:3 *Everlasting love for us*

Philippians 4:19 *Supplies our needs*

Isaiah 26:3 *He gives us perfect peace*

Hebrews 13:5 *He will never leave us*

Hebrews 13:6 *We have no need to fear man because God is for us + is our helper.*

 7. <u>Philippians 4:6 and 7</u>. God's formula to defeat worry includes three steps. What are they (v. 6)?

Don't worry about anything
Pray about everything
Be thankful

This is my version of God's formula to overcome worry in Philippians 4:6 and 7.

Don't worry about anything.
Pray about everything.
Thank the Lord for everything.
And you will have peace.

8. The apostle Paul is an excellent example of one who had inner joy when external circumstances were against him. Where was Paul when he wrote the book of Philippians? Read Philippians 1:13, 14, and 20.

9. Philippians 4:11. What do the three words "I have learned" tell you about contentment?

Contentment is learned, not just given at time of salvation

10. Philippians 4:13.
   (a) What is the difference between trying to live the Christian life in our own strength or living it in God's strength? See also 1 Corinthians 15:57. *We will fail if we try to do things without God*

   (b) For us to do the "all things" that God wants to empower us to do, what must we do first? Read Ephesians 4:22–24.
   Get rid of our old self

"As we immerse ourselves in the Word, the Holy Spirit strengthens our 'inner man' (Ephesians 3:16). The Spirit's power through the Word could be compared to dipping a tea bag into hot water. The longer the tea bag stays in the water, the stronger [the tea] becomes. The more time we spend in the Word, the more strength is infused into us by the Holy Spirit, Who lives in us."[2]

Second Corinthians 3:18 says that as we behold the glory of the Lord, we are "changed into the same image from glory to glory, even as by the Spirit of the Lord." The Spirit of God takes the Word of God and changes us to become like the Son of God—Jesus Christ.

11. Philippians 4:19.
   (a) Since God has promised to provide for us, why do we sometimes feel He is not supplying our needs?

(b) Relate a time in your life when you got your needs and your greeds (wants) mixed up. What needless financial and emotional stress did you bring on yourself?

12. 2 Timothy 1:7.
   (a) If fear doesn't come from God, where does it come from?
   Satan
   (b) How does 1 John 4:18 describe fear?
   Fear involves torment

13. Isaiah 43:2.
   (a) What do floodwaters and fire picture in this verse?
   trials

   (b) What is the significance of the words "passest through" and "walkest through"? *We will make it!*

Warren Wiersbe has said, "We must keep in mind that God controls the storms. . . . He knows when we go into the storm, He watches over us in the storm, and He can bring us out of the storm when His purposes have been fulfilled. At the right time, He can say to the storm, 'Hush, be still!' and make it a great calm (Mark 4:39). . . . God does speak to us out of the storms of life. . . . The important thing is that we trust Him and keep our ears tuned for His message."[3]

14. Luke 1:37; Isaiah 26:3. When we are facing impossibilities, how can fixing our minds on God's promises instead of our problems result in peace? *He has told us He will be with us.*

15. Hebrews 13:5. Why do we often feel God is not near? Who has moved? *We lose our focus + drift away*

16. Job 23:10. How does this verse give you confidence that God has everything under control in your life and that everything is running right on schedule?

17. Jeremiah 31:3. Why do we have a hard time understanding everlasting, or unconditional, love?

We can't have unconditional love in our earthly bodies

18. Psalm 18:30. Think through the three truths presented in this verse; then write the verse in your words.

19. Psalm 91:1, 2. Why is the "shadow of the Almighty" such a safe place to dwell? Also read the last part of James 1:17.

Can we stay on top of our circumstances and not live under them? Yes, as we wait upon the Lord for His strength day by day. "But thanks be to God, which giveth us the victory through our Lord Jesus Christ" (1 Corinthians 15:57). Use the verses you have studied in this lesson to start building your ark of faith. I guarantee that it works, and having an ark of faith will save you from disaster.

FROM MY HEART

Having lived in Florida for over thirty years, I have learned to be prepared in hurricane season—June through November. I know I need to stockpile certain things or keep them on hand during that time. If a hurricane should come inland, we would be without electricity and water for several days; we need to be prepared before the storm comes. So it is in our life of faith. We know there will be storms and trials; we need to be prepared before they come. How can we prepare ourselves? Build an ark of faith—fortify our lives with the Word of God.

I've been building my ark of faith for many years now, but sometimes my faith wavers. When I begin to fear I can't endure some trial, I think of something Corrie Ten Boom's father told her when she spoke of her fear of what she might do if she were tortured and put in a concentration camp for illegally harboring Jews. When she imagined how bad it could be, she said to her father, "What if I deny my Lord?" He answered, "Remember when you were a little child and you took a train ride? When did I give you the ticket? Was it two weeks in advance?" She replied, "No, it was when I got on the train." He said, "When you get on the train, the ticket will be there."

I need not fear the future. I've built my ark of faith; the ticket will be there.

FROM YOUR HEART

Which of the verses we studied were most helpful to you? Begin today to memorize those verses. Set a goal to memorize one a week. Then memorize the other verses on the "Why Sink When You Can Swim?" list (pp. 53, 54). It is hard to learn the verses when the storm comes; your mind is filled with your problems. You have to have the verses in your heart and mind before the wind begins to blow. Add other verses to the list as you come across them in your Bible reading. Personalize the list; make it your own ark of faith.

Notes

1. George Muller. Quoted by Mrs. Charles Cowman, *Springs in the Valley* (Grand Rapids: Zondervan Publishing House, 1968), 248.

2. Juanita Purcell, *The Secret of Contentment* (Schaumburg, IL: Regular Baptist Press, 2006), 34.

3. Warren W. Wiersbe, *When Life Falls Apart* (Grand Rapids: Fleming H. Revell, 1998), 59, 60.

WHY SINK WHEN YOU CAN SWIM VERSES

(Cut this page from your book on the dotted line and place it in the front of your Bible.)

Genesis 18:25—"Shall not the Judge [Ruler] of all the earth do right?"

Job 23:10—"But he knoweth the way that I take: when he hath tried [tested] me, I shall come forth as gold."

Psalm 18:30—"As for God, his way is perfect: the word of the LORD is tried [proved]: he is a buckler to all those that trust in him."

Psalm 31:15—"My times are in thy hand."

Psalm 34:4—"I sought the LORD, and he heard me, and delivered me from all my fears."

Psalm 37:23—"The steps of a good man are ordered by the LORD: and he delighteth in his way."

Psalm 46:10—"Be still, and know that I am God."

Psalm 91:1, 2—"He that dwelleth in the secret place of the most High shall abide under the shadow of the Almighty. I will say of the LORD, He is my refuge and my fortress: my God; in him will I trust."

Proverbs 3:5, 6—"Trust in the LORD with all thine heart; and lean not unto thine own understanding. In all thy ways acknowledge him, and he shall direct thy paths."

Proverbs 17:22—"A merry heart doeth good like a medicine: but a broken spirit drieth the bones."

Isaiah 26:3—"Thou wilt keep him in perfect peace, whose mind is stayed on thee: because he trusteth in thee."

Isaiah 40:31—"But they that wait upon the LORD shall renew their strength; they shall mount up with wings as eagles; they shall run, and not be weary; and they shall walk, and not faint."

Isaiah 43:2—"When thou passest through the waters, I will be with thee; and through the rivers, they shall not overflow thee: when thou walkest through the fire, thou shalt not be burned; neither shall the flame kindle upon thee."

Isaiah 50:10—"Who is among you that feareth the LORD, that obeyeth the voice of his servant, that walketh in darkness, and hath no light? Let him trust in the name of the LORD, and stay upon his God."

Jeremiah 29:11—"For I know the thoughts that I think toward you, saith the LORD, thoughts of peace, and not of evil, to give you an expected end."

Jeremiah 31:3—"Yea, I have loved thee with an everlasting love."

Jeremiah 33:3—"Call unto me, and I will answer thee, and [show] thee great and mighty things, which thou knowest not."

Habakkuk 3:17, 18—"Although the fig tree shall not blossom, neither shall fruit be in the vines; the labour of the olive shall fail, and the fields shall yield no meat; the flock shall be cut off from the fold, and there shall be no herd in the stalls: Yet I will rejoice in the LORD, I will joy in the God of my salvation."

Luke 1:37—"For with God nothing shall be impossible."

Roman 8:28, 29—"And we know that all things work together for good to them that love God, to them who are the called according to his purpose. For whom he did foreknow, he also did predestinate to be conformed to the image of his Son."

1 Corinthians 10:13—"There hath no temptation taken you but such as is common to man: but God is faithful, who will not suffer you to be tempted above that ye are able; but will with the temptation also make a way to escape, that ye may be able to bear it."

Philippians 4:4—"Rejoice in the Lord alway: and again I say, Rejoice."

Philippians 4:6, 7—"Be careful [anxious] for nothing; but in every thing by prayer and supplication with thanksgiving let your requests be made known unto God. And the peace of God, which passeth all understanding, shall keep your hearts and minds through Christ Jesus."

Philippians 4:11—"Not that I speak in respect of want: for I have learned, in whatsoever state I am, therewith to be content."

Philippians 4:13—"I can do all things through Christ which strengtheneth me."

Philippians 4:19—"But my God shall supply all your need according to his riches in glory by Christ Jesus."

1 Thessalonians 5:18—"In every thing give thanks: for this is the will of God in Christ Jesus concerning you."

2 Timothy 1:7—"For God hath not given us the spirit of fear; but of power, and of love, and of a sound mind."

Hebrews 13:5, 6—"He hath said, I will never leave thee, nor forsake thee. So that we may boldly say, The Lord is my helper, and I will not fear what man shall do unto me."

James 1:2, 3—"My brethren, count it all joy when ye fall into divers [various] temptations; knowing this, that the trying of your faith worketh patience."

1 Peter 5:7—"Casting all your care upon him; for he careth for you."

We Can All Get Down in the Dumps

"Hear me speedily, O LORD: my spirit faileth: hide not thy face from me, lest I be like unto them that go down into the pit" (Psalm 143:7).

When our trials go on and on with no relief in sight, they may begin to wear us down mentally, emotionally, and sometimes physically.

Elijah is a good example for us to consider. He had a literal mountaintop experience that is recorded in 1 Kings 18. After three years of no rain in Israel, Elijah confronted wicked King Ahab and the prophets of Baal on Mount Carmel.

1. What challenge did Elijah give to the prophets of Baal, the false god whom the Israelites were worshiping (vv. 22–24)?

Fire from Heaven

2. What happened (vv. 26–38)?

These kinds of experiences are wonderful, but they can also be emotionally exhausting. Elijah went from a mountaintop experience full of faith to a desert experience full of fear in one day (1 Kings 19:1–3).

Elijah would agree with Alexander, a little boy who said he was having "a terrible, horrible, no good, very bad day." We can all get down in the dumps just like Elijah did. Any one of a multitude of negative circumstances can push us over the edge and send us into a pit of despair. We may wish we could just die and get out of our misery. However, if we stay in the pit too long, we will end up with PMS—Poor Me Syndrome.

I find I am most susceptible to the blahs or self-pity when I get myself in a flurry of activities with no time to rest in between. I also experience self-pity if it seems trials never end. One passes, and then another comes right after it.

3. Christ did not promise that we would never hurt. What is His promise as recorded in Matthew 11:28?

Rest

4. Why is it hard to rest when our hearts are broken and we hurt so badly? focus isn't on God

God knew there would be times when we would be burdened with trials, but He wants to give us rest so we can get up and finish our journey. It's all right to hurt—but not for too long.

5. Read Psalm 42:5 and 9–11. If we don't get out of the dumps, what can happen? We become defeated. + discouraged

6. Long periods of discouragement can lead to self-pity. To what can self-pity lead? Read 1 Kings 19:4 and Psalm 134:7. 143:7 thoughts of suicide

Elisabeth Elliot has said, "I know of nothing more paralyzing, more deadly, than self-pity. It is a death that has no resurrection, a sink-hole from which no rescuing hand can drag you because you have chosen to sink."[1]

7. Elijah had had it; he was ready to die (1 Kings 19:4). Read Psalm 55:4 and 6. When do we most long for Heaven?

James Dyet made this observation about Elijah—and God: "Strange how the mind runs offtrack when the blahs hit! We think and say things that don't make any sense. Elijah asked God to take away his life. Why the marathon run through Israel, Judah, and into the desert? If he had really wanted to die, he could have stayed in Israel. Jezebel would have gladly obliged his request. It's a good thing God doesn't grant everything we ask of Him."[2]

8. In times of trials sometimes our first response is just to get away from everyone and everything. Read Psalm 55:22. What did the psalmist say is a better course in times of trials?

Sometimes we may even want to get away from God. Nancy Missler confides: "When everything around me crashed and totally contradicted all that I thought the Lord had promised, instead of my faith becoming 'sight' and giving me hope, I became disappointed, resentful and even bitter towards God. It's a horrible place to be, because in this state, we're unable to move forward, and yet, we can't turn back either. Hope in God is critical. As Scripture declares, 'Where there is no vision [or hope for the future] the people perish . . .' and 'hope deferred makes the heart sick.' (Proverbs 29:18, 13:12)."[3]

9. Read Job 23:10.
   (a) What is the promise in this verse?
   The trial is to make us better

   (b) Why is it hard to believe this promise when our trial has led to despair? *Because we are looking at the trial*

Doctors Minirth and Meier list the following five major symptoms of depression: (1) sad affect (moodiness); (2) painful thinking; (3) physical symptoms; (4) anxiety or agitation; (5) delusional thinking.[4]

10. Read Psalm 42:4 and 5. How would you describe the psalmist's painful thinking?

11. How can painful thinking lead to withdrawal from people?

James Jauncey explains: "Such things as worry, conflict, tension or guilt, consume vast quantities of nervous energy. This may steadily eat into nervous capital until it is practically exhausted. Suddenly there simply isn't enough nervous energy left to control the impulses of the nervous system, or to control the emotions or the will. This action is much like that of an automobile battery. When it falls below a certain point, it just gives up entirely."[5]

12. Read Psalm 25:15. How could this verse help a person who is experiencing painful thinking to refocus?

Go back to worship

Mark Batterson tells what he does to refocus: "When I get into a spiritual or emotional slump, it's usually because I've zoomed in on a problem. I'm fixating on . . . my circumstances. . . . So how do we zoom out? The one-word answer is worship. . . . Worship is zooming out and refocusing on the big picture. . . . Worship is forgetting about what's wrong with you and remembering what's right with God. . . . It renews your mind. And it enables you to find something good to praise God about even when everything seems to be going wrong."[6]

13. Depression is often called a "dark pit." When people get into this state of mind, they often lose hope that things will ever be better. What words in Psalm 42:5 and 11 indicate that the psalmist was very discouraged, or in despair, but not in a pit of depression?

Hope in God

14. Read Psalm 42:5 and 11 again. Also read Psalm 43:5. What did the psalmist mean when he said God was "the health of my countenance"?

15. What physical problems can depression cause?

16. We know depression can cause physical problems. We also know physical problems can trigger depression. What are some of those problems?

When we feel depressed, a trip to the doctor may be in order. "What triggers periods of depression? Some supersaints insist that depression is caused exclusively by a lack of faith. 'If you would just trust the Lord, you wouldn't get depressed,' they tell us. But sometimes an underactive thyroid or some other physical problem can trigger depression, and all the sermons in the world won't make it go away. A medical checkup may be more helpful than hearing Job-like counselors quote Scripture."[7]

17. When we realize we are experiencing the painful-thinking symptom of depression, what must we do with our minds? Read Isaiah 26:3.   Trust + Focus

18. If you have had occasion to use the "Why Sink When You Can Swim?" verses on pages 53 and 54, how has God's Word helped you?

FROM MY HEART

I have found that the fastest way to get out of the dumps (the blahs) is to admit to myself and others, if needed, how I feel. Then I must ask myself if I really want to stay in the dumps. The next thing is to try to figure out why I am there. Is this a physical, spiritual, or emotional battle? Was it triggered by a physical problem? If the cause is spiritual, I know what to do about that. If the cause is physical, I go to the doctor.

Emotional problems are the most difficult to deal with, but the root of those problems may also be physical or spiritual. Emotional problems, if not dealt with in the early stages, might require outside help from a pastor or counselor.

I have found in my own life that when I am on an emotional roller coaster, it is usually the result of negative thinking, I have labeled negative thinking as "stinkin-thinkin." I keep reminding myself that I can't feel discouraged unless I am thinking discouraging thoughts.

Depression is a downward spiral that starts with disappointment, moves to discouragement, becomes despair, and ends in depression. The next time you are down in the dumps, do this self-test; it could keep you out of the pit of depression.

- Admit you feel down.
- Do you want to stay there?
- How did you get down?
- Is your problem physical, spiritual, or emotional?
- What are you going to do to get back up?

We can all get down in the dumps, but we make the choice whether or not we want to stay there.

FROM YOUR HEART

How did this lesson help you personally? Did you get a better understanding of people who suffer from depression or other emotional problems? How will the self-test help you the next time you feel down in the dumps? Are you memorizing the "Why Sink When You Can Swim?" verses?

Notes

1. Elisabeth Elliot, *Facing the Death of Someone You Love* (Westchester, IL: Good New Publishers, 1982).

2. Dyet, 42.

3. Missler, 214.

4. Frank B. Minirth and Paul D. Meier, *Happiness Is a Choice* (Grand Rapids: Baker Book House, 1978), 24–27.

5. James H. Jauncey, *Above Ourselves* (Grand Rapids: Zondervan Publishing House, 1964), 92.

6. Mark Batterson, *In a Pit with a Lion on a Snowy Day* (Colorado Springs: Multnomah Books, 2006), 66, 67.

7. Dyet, 41.

Trials Teach Us
How to Be Comforters

"Who comforteth us in all our tribulation, that we may be able to comfort them which are in any trouble, by the comfort wherewith we ourselves are comforted of God" (2 Corinthians 1:4).

I have often felt my life was suddenly falling apart and things would never be the same again. Many times I have struggled with the feeling that God had forgotten me. I've found myself saying, "If God can do anything, why is He doing nothing?" But, looking back, I see He was doing something when it seemed He was doing nothing. While I was waiting for Him to change other people or circumstances, He was changing me.

In times of trial, I need all the encouragement I can get. If I need encouragement in tough times, I know others need it as well. I pray that God will help me share with hurting people some of the things He has taught me when I've been hurting.

We have four great sources of comfort available to us, resources far greater than man can provide: God the Father, God the Son, God the Holy Spirit, and the Scriptures. As God uses these resources in our lives, we are then able to comfort others.

The Father's Comfort

1. Read Psalm 46:1–3. How does God the Father comfort us?

   Refuge and strength
   Very present help in trouble

2. Read Psalm 46:10. What does our Heavenly Father want us to do to receive His comfort?

   "Be still + know that I am God"

Likening life to a play, Warren Wiersbe has said: "The God I worship doesn't have to be brought on stage to solve problems. He wrote the script! For that matter, He is in charge of the drama, and He will see to it that everything works out right because He is also one of the actors in the play."[1]

3. Read Isaiah 66:13. How did God the Father comfort the Israelites?

4. Read 2 Thessalonians 2:16 and 17. How long will God's comfort be available to His children? *Everlasting Consolation*

Changing metaphors, Pastor Wiersbe observed that "God's promises aren't celestial life preservers that He throws out to strangers in the storm. They are expressions of His love and care, given to His children who walk with Him and seek to obey Him. . . . We will have an easier time trusting God in the darkness if we have walked with Him in the light."[2]

The Son's Comfort

5. Read Hebrews 4:15. How is God the Son able to comfort us?
He can sympathize with us because He has experienced life's troubles

6. Why should we not say, "No one understands how I feel"? In addition to Hebrews 4:15, look at Hebrews 2:14–16.
Comforts us when He doesn't comfort Angels.

The Spirit's Comfort

7. Read John 14:16–18. Describe the comfort of the Holy Spirit.
He dwells with us + in us: forever

8. Read Ephesians 3:16. How does this verse describe the work of Spirit in our lives? *Strengthen us in the inner man*

Consider these encouraging words from Pastor Wiersbe: "The Spirit of God is not distant from you, sending you advice; He is living in you and giving you the strength and wisdom you need for the decisions of life. Trust Him, wait for His help, and know that He will never fail you. In due time, the Comforter will minister to your needs and encourage your heart."[3]

The Comfort of the Scriptures

9. Read Romans 15:4. What does God's Word do for us?

Gives us hope
Instruction
Patience
Comfort

Many books are written to comfort believers, but no book can give comfort like the Bible. Here are some Scripture passages to comfort and help you in times of trial and trouble.

- If you have no one to talk to about your problems, read 1 Peter 5:7.
- If you are worried and full of fear, read Psalm 23.
- If you are disappointed and discouraged, read Psalm 43:5.
- If you are having trouble loving others as you should, read 1 Corinthians 13.
- If you are unable to forgive those who have hurt you, read Matthew 6:14 and 15 and Matthew 18:21 and 22.
- If you are afraid to die, read John 14:1–3.
- If you are not sure you have eternal life, read John 3:1–16 and Romans 3:23, 5:8, 6:23, 10:9 and 10 and 13.

"To profit most from the adversity, we should bring the Word of God to bear upon the situation. We should ask God to bring to our attention pertinent passages of Scripture. . . . As we seek to relate the Scriptures to our adversities, we'll find we will not only profit from the circumstances themselves, but we will gain new insight into the Scriptures. . . . Adversity enhances the teaching of God's Word and makes it more profitable to us."[4]

Comforting Others

10. When a person is hurting, what one thing do you think she needs most from someone else?

Listener, Comfort
Understanding

The fact that people will pay hundreds of dollars for someone to just listen to them for an hour should alert us to the importance of having someone to talk to when we are hurting.

11. Why is talking to someone so important?

Another prospective

12. Read Psalm 69:20 and Ecclesiastes 4:1. How does a person feel if he has no counselor? *Hopeless*

13. Pastors and counselors are often good comforters. Read 2 Corinthians 1:4. Who else can be a good comforter?
Other believers

Someone has noted that "suddenly or gradually, when one's world has been broken, the question of hope usually arises. Is there a tomorrow? Will there be another chance? Is the damage permanent? Do new starts exist? Can this broken world ever be rebuilt?"[5]

"Broken-world" people were as common in Bible times as they are today. One's world may be broken due to tragedy, loss, or other circumstances. Broken-world people may need to experience God's forgiveness before they can go on with their lives. All broken-world people need our encouragement and comfort.

14. Read about the lives of some Biblical broken-world people. What was the cause of their brokenness and how was it resolved?

    (a) David. Read 2 Samuel 11:1–5 and Psalm 51:1–4 and 12.

    Cause: *Bathsheba*

    Resolution: *Prayed + asking to be forgiven + restored to the joy of His Salvation*

    (b) Naomi. Read Ruth 1:1–5, 20–22 and 4:13–17.

    Cause: *Death of Sons*

Resolution: *followed Gods plan for her*

(c) Joseph. Read Genesis 37:18–28 and 50:20.

Cause: *betrayed by brother*

Resolution: *God turned it around + blessed him*

(d) Mary and Martha. Read John 11:1–4, 19–45.

Cause: *death of Lazarus*

Resolution: *Jesus showed His glory by resurrecting*

15. What is the difference between sympathizing with someone and empathizing with that person?

Sorrow – Sympathy
experienced it – empathy

16. How can the trials we endure furnish us with nourishment for other troubled hearts? Read 2 Corinthians 1:3–5.

"The heart that has not suffered has little comfort to give to those who weep and suffer in a sorrowing world, because sympathy is born of experience. We are only capable of comforting one another, when, individually, we know the joy of divine comfort."[6]

Maybe you aren't far enough along in your trial that you can help someone else. Is your heart still hurting and no one seems to care? Do you need a safe, secure, secret place to hide and heal? There is only one place to go: "under the shadow of the Almighty" (Psalm 91:1, 2). He is our strength, mighty rock, fortress, and stronghold. He is the God of all comfort. Our God is a very present help in the time of need. He has not left us comfortless.

Does Jesus care when my heart is pained
Too deeply for mirth and song;
As the burdens press, and the cares distress,
And the way grows weary and long?

O yes, He cares—I know He cares!
His heart is touched with my grief:
When the days are weary, the long nights dreary,
I know my Savior cares.[7]

FROM MY HEART

I still have a long way to go to be a good comforter, but God has taught me so much over the years. Each trial I have passed through has given me fresh insights on how to comfort others. Often I share the "Why Sink When You Can Swim?" verses. Sometimes I use Charles Allen's prescription for hurting people. Think of it as a prescription from a doctor.

Read Psalm 23 five times a day for seven days.
Must be taken as prescribed.
Read it first thing in the morning.
Read it after breakfast.
Read it after lunch.
Read it after dinner.
Read it before bedtime.[8]

What wonderful resources I have to comfort me! I have the Trinity and God's Word to comfort me "from the inside out" and other people who comfort me "from the outside in." You have these same resources if you have a personal relationship with Jesus Christ. If you don't have this relationship, you can call upon the Lord right now and receive Him as your Savior. Please read the Bible verses on pages 5 and 6. You can also talk to your Bible study leader about this important decision.

FROM YOUR HEART

How have the members of the Trinity and the Word of God encouraged you "from the inside out"?

Do you have a friend who comforts you "from the outside in"? What lessons have you learned that you could share with someone else?

Notes

1. Wiersbe, *When Life Falls Apart*, 79.

2. Ibid., 83, 84.

3. Warren W. Wiersbe, *The Bumps Are What You Climb On* (Grand Rapids: Baker Book House, 1980), 94, 95.

4. Jerry Bridges, *Trusting God Even When Life Hurts* (Colorado Springs: Navpress, 1988), 178.

5. Gordon MacDonald, *Rebuilding Your Broken World* (Nashville: Thomas Nelson Publishers, 1988), 25.

6. Herbert Lockyer, *Dark Threads the Weaver Needs* (Old Tappan, NJ: Fleming H. Revell Co., 1979), 111.

7. J. Lincoln Hall.

8. Summarized from Charles L. Allen, *God's Psychiatry* (Old Tappan, NJ: Fleming H. Revell Co., 1953).

L E S S O N 1 0

Keep Looking Up— Not around You

"Mine eyes are ever toward the LORD" (Psalm 25:15).

I t is not enough just to endure trials and even learn from them. God wants us to have joy in the midst of our trials. The psalmist prayed, "Make us glad according to the days wherein thou hast afflicted us, and the years wherein we have seen evil" (Psalm 90:15). David said God had "turned for me my mourning into dancing: thou hast put off my sackcloth, and girded me with gladness" (Psalm 30:11).

Before we answer the question, How can we have joy in the midst of trials? we need to know what real joy is.

Defining Joy

1. How do you define joy? *feeling of well-being*

2. Where is real joy found? Read Psalm 16:11.
   In the presence of the Lord

3. Read Habakkuk 3:17 and 18.
   (a) What kind of dire circumstances did the prophet enumerate?
   No harvest, flocks, herd

   (b) What was the prophet's response to those circumstances?
   "I will rejoice in the Lord"

Tim Hansel wrote: "Pain is inevitable, but misery is optional. We cannot avoid pain, but we can avoid joy. God . . . will allow us to be as

69

miserable as we want to be. . . . Joy is simple (not to be confused with easy). At any moment in life we have at least two options, and one of them is to choose an attitude of gratitude, a posture of grace, a commitment to joy."[1]

4. How is joy produced in our lives? Read Galatians 5:22 and 23.

Fruit of the Spirit

James Dyet noticed these truths about joy: "Joy cannot be manufactured; the Holy Spirit produces it. We must not make the mistake of thinking that pumped-up elation is true joy. Joy isn't worked up; it is sent down. . . . Insecure circumstances cannot destroy real joy because it is anchored in Christ. Real joy doesn't depend on who we are but on Who Christ is. . . . Joy is lasting because the One Who shares His joy with us is eternal."[2]

5. What circumstances or people in your life tend to rob you of joy? Why do you lose your joy?

Joy comes as we walk in the Spirit (Galatians 5:16), but we can lose our joy if we get our eyes off Christ and on our circumstances. An old hymn admonishes us to "turn your eyes upon Jesus, Look full in His wonderful face." How can we joy despite our circumstances? Keep looking up—not around us!

Looking Up

6. Psalm 25:15 says, "Mine eyes are ever toward the LORD." What does it mean to keep our eyes on the Lord instead of our circumstances?

Look at things the way Jesus would. Dwell on God's promises.

7. Read Psalms 41:9 and 55:4–6. Why is it so important that we keep our eyes on Christ and not on our circumstances or on other people? *Circumstances can overwhelm us. People hurt us*

8. What truth is taught in this couplet: "Two men looked out from prison bars; The one saw mud; the other saw stars"?

9. Read Matthew 14:22–33. What happened to Peter when he got his eyes on his circumstances rather than Christ?

Began to sink

10. How does Peter's experience apply to us?

"What Christian hasn't faced a tumultuous, seemingly hopeless situation?" asks James Dyet. "I have been there and, like Peter, I tried to approach God and keep my eyes on Him, but I failed. The dreadful circumstances raging around me overwhelmed my faith and stole my attention away from God. I could feel myself sinking. All I could do was cry out, 'Lord, save me!' But it was also the best thing I could do."[3]

11. What does James 1:8 say about a person who tries to keep her eyes on Christ and her circumstances at the same time?

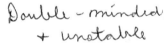
Double-minded + unstable

12. Some trials may be the result of financial problems. If we get our eyes on making money instead of living for Christ, what can happen? Read 1 Timothy 6:10.

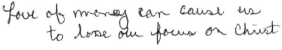
Love of money can cause us to lose our focus on Christ

13. Evaluate the following statement by John W. Gardner: "If happiness could be found in having material things, and in being able to indulge yourself in things that you consider pleasurable, then we, in America, would be deliriously happy. We would be telling one

another frequently of our unparalleled bliss, rather than trading tranquilizer prescriptions."[4]

Learning Contentment

14. (a) What is contentment?

Being at peace

(b) Read Philippians 4:11 and 12. What is the source of contentment? *God*

Warren Wiersbe defines contentment this way: "Contentment is having that spiritual artesian well within so that you don't have to run to the broken cisterns of the world to get what you need. The power of Christ in the inner man is all we need for the demands of life. Resources on the outside, such as friends and counselors and encouragements, are only helpful as they strengthen our resources on the inside."[5]

The discontent person does have what she doesn't want and does not have what she does want. A discontent person suffers the loss of peace and joy.

15. Contentment is not a product of strong self-discipline or willpower. Read Philippians 4:13. What is available to believers to help us learn to be content? *"I can do all things through Christ who strengthens me"*

16. If you graded yourself on contentment, what grade would you get?

To have joy in the midst of trials, we need to keep our eyes off our circumstances and on Christ. We need to learn to be content. We do this by maintaining our spiritual lives.

17. What does it mean to maintain one's spiritual life? Read 2 Timothy 2:15; 1 John 1:9; Galatians 5:16.

Study the Word
Confess our sins
Walk in the Spirit

18. Why should maintaining one's spiritual life be a daily activity? Read Psalms 5:3; 55:17; 88:9; 145:2.

19. What method do you use for daily Bible reading?

I discovered a Bible reading method called "Partners." The thought behind the name is I do my part and God will do His part. Read one psalm a day and write your observation by each of the words in the acrostic. You can break the longer psalms into smaller passages.[6]

P raise God for Who He is

A dmit my sins and feelings

R equest from God what I need

T hank God for what He is doing

Laughing

Here is another tip to get your eyes off of your circumstances. Find something to laugh about.

20. Read Proverbs 17:22. What did Solomon say about laughter?

Tim Hansel has put it this way: "Humor has the unshakable ability to break life up into little pieces and make it liveable. Laughter adds richness, texture, and color to otherwise ordinary days."[7]

If you are under a lot of stress and can't find anything funny to laugh about, read the item below. It is good for a hearty laugh.

STRESS DIET
Breakfast

½ grapefruit

1 slice of whole wheat bread

8 ounces skim milk

Lunch

4 ounces broiled chicken breast
1 cup steamed zucchini
1 Oreo cookie
1 cup herb tea

Mid-afternoon snack

Rest of the package of Oreo cookies
One quart of Rocky Road ice cream
One jar of hot fudge

Dinner

Two loaves of garlic bread
Large pepperoni and mushroom pizza
One liter of Coke
Three candy bars
Entire frozen cheesecake eaten directly from the freezer

DIET TIPS

1. If no one sees you eat it, it has no calories.
2. If you drink a diet soda with a candy bar, the calories will cancel out.
3. Calories don't count if you eat with someone and you both eat the same thing.
4. Pieces of cookies contain no calories. The process of breaking causes calorie leakage.

FROM MY HEART

When life's circumstances are good, it is easy to sing, "God is so good," and to keep my eyes on Christ and all His blessings. But circumstances can change with one phone call. Suddenly life becomes overwhelming; my song and my joy are gone; and my eyes are not on the Lord. I need to refocus: get my eyes back on the Lord and off the circumstances. (I'll pull out the "Why Sink When You Can Swim?" verses.) I can't say I always do this right away, but I am making progress. I have learned that the key to having joy in the midst of trials is to focus ON promises and OFF problems. Try it—it works!

FROM YOUR HEART

How do you rate yourself on the joy and contentment scale? What did you learn from this lesson that will help you the next time you feel overwhelmed with your circumstances? If you do not have a meaningful devotional life, what steps will you take to get back on track?

Notes

1. Tim Hansel, *You Gotta Keep Dancin'* (Elgin, IL: David C. Cook Publishing Co., 1985), 55.

2. Dyet, 74.

3. Ibid., 83.

4. Quoted by Gail MacDonald, *Keep Climbing*, 65.

5. Wiersbe, *The Bumps Are What You Climb On*, 132.

6. The daily devotional book *Be Still My Child* by Juanita Purcell may be used to supplement your Bible study. The book goes through the entire book of Psalms in one year. To order, go to www.RBPstore.org.

7. Hansel, 82.

Live One Day at a Time

*"This one thing I do, forgetting those things which are be-
hind, and reaching forth unto those things which are before,
I press toward the mark for the prize of the high calling of
God in Christ Jesus" (Philippians 3:13, 14).*

To have joy in the midst of our trials, we must learn to live one day
at a time—and that day is today. We must forget yesterday and not
worry about tomorrow.

1. What is the difference between an "if only-er" and a "what if-er"?

Looking back   *Not trusting*

Many of us have difficulty living one day at a time; we let guilt and
lack of forgiveness cloud our memories of yesterday, and we worry about
tomorrow. Let's look more closely at guilt, forgiveness, and worry.

Guilt

2. How would you define these two concepts?

Destructive guilt — *Destroys life*

Constructive guilt — *Can help us change*

3. If a person has constructive guilt over something in her past, what
should she do? Read Psalm 51:1–4 and 1 John 1:9.

Confess it to the Lord + then anyone who needs it.

4. If a person has destructive guilt over something in her past, what
should she do? Read Philippians 3:13. *Pray to forget it.*

Some people say they can accept God's forgiveness, but they can't forgive themselves. God never tells us to forgive ourselves—just accept His forgiveness. The only time we should feel guilty is when we sin. I like this description of sin, "Sin is the failure to obey a command of God, whether by not doing what He requires or by doing what He forbids."[1]

    5. What "if only" have you been dwelling on that has caused destructive guilt in your life? What do you need to tell yourself? Read Jeremiah 31:34 again.

At times we need to change things, but at other times we need to "write them in the sand, letting the waves of God's mercy wash over those words and forever eradicate them."[2]

Forgiveness

    6. Why must we have God's forgiveness? Read Psalm 103:3, 4, 12, and 13. (For other verses on God's forgiveness, see Psalms 86:5; 130:3, 4; Isaiah 55:7; Micah 7:18; and Mark 2:7.)

    7. We know our omniscient God does not forget. What did God mean when He said He would "not remember thy sins" (Isaiah 43:25)?

    8. Who accuses us of our sin before God? Read Revelation 12:9.

                                                  Satan

    9. God never tells us to forgive ourselves; however He tells us many times to forgive others. Why must we forgive? Read Ephesians 4:32 and Colossians 3:12 and 13.   *Because He forgives us*

10. How can we forgive a person who doesn't deserve it and who has no intention of changing his or her behavior? Read Isaiah 40:31 and Philippians 4:13.

Exchange our strength for His strength

11. Consider these Biblical examples of forgiveness. In each case, what was done to the person, and how did that person evidence forgiveness?
Joseph (Genesis 37:12–28; 50:17–21)

Stephen (Acts 6:9—7:2; 7:51–60)

Ephesians 4:31+32

Jesus (Luke 23:20–34)

12. Is there someone you need to forgive? Parent? mate? boss? God? others? What do you need to forgive?

Write the initials of the one(s) you need to forgive on these lines. Would you ask God to help you write FORGIVEN across their initials? _____
_____

Forgiveness is an act of the will. No one can do it for us. It is something we choose to do and keep doing. Just as we need daily bread, we need daily forgiveness. We also need to pray daily that we will have the grace to forgive others as God has forgiven us.

Ken Sande explains that "through forgiveness God tears down the walls that our sins have built, and he opens the way for a renewed relationship with him. This is exactly what we must do if we are to forgive as the Lord forgives us. . . . Therefore, forgiveness may be described as a decision to make four promises:

'I will not dwell on this incident.'

'I will not bring up this incident again and use it against you.'

'I will not talk to others about this incident.'

'I will not let this incident stand between us or hinder our personal relationship.' "[3]

Worry

13. You may not be plagued with guilt or an unforgiving spirit, but you may be a "what if-er." Do you worry about tomorrow? What's the difference between normal precaution and fretful worry?

14. I once read that only 8 percent of things we worry about ever come to pass. Read Philippians 4:6 and 7 and Matthew 6:31, 32, and 34. What are we saying to God when we worry?

"We make our lives insupportably complex by disobeying Jesus' command to take no thought for tomorrow," writes Elisabeth Elliot. "Planning for tomorrow, when planning is necessary and possible, belongs properly to today. Worry about tomorrow belongs nowhere. The Lord gives us daily, not weekly, bread. He gives strength according to our days, not our years. The work, the suffering, the joy are given according to His careful measure."[4]

15. What is another word for worry in James 4:17?

Said the Robin to the Sparrow:
"I should really like to know
Why these anxious human beings
Rush about and worry so."

Said the Sparrow to the Robin:
"Friend, I think that it must be
That they have no heavenly Father
Such as cares for you and me."[5]

16. What physical problems can worry cause?

17. Read Philippians 4. Find at least eleven ways to help defeat the
worry habit.

Verse 4 *Rejoice in the Lord always*

Verse 5

Verse 6

Verse 6

Verse 6 *Be thankful*

Verse 8

Verse 9

Verse 10

Verse 11

Verse 13

Verse 19

18. List some practical ways to put the truths of Philippians 4 into
practice in your own life.

We can have joy in the midst of our trials, but not until we get rid of
guilt and an unforgiving spirit. And not until we stop worrying and learn
to live one day at a time.

FROM MY HEART

Sometimes I have a hard time with forgiveness. When that happens, I need to remind myself how many times God has forgiven me. But most of all, I must keep forgiving because I value my relationship with the Lord more than any other relationship. If I won't forgive others, then I lose fellowship with Him—and I don't want that to happen.

Forgiveness is hard, but living worry-free seems even harder. Times keep changing and getting worse, but our God stays the same—yesterday, today, and forever (Hebrews 13:8). He has told us repeatedly in His Word, "Fret not." God knows everything about me, even the number of hairs on my head (Matthew 10:30)! He has also told me I am in Christ's hand, and His hand is over Christ's hand (John 10:27–29). Nothing can touch me unless God allows it. I must learn to trust Him!

FROM YOUR HEART

What did you learn about guilt, forgiveness, and worry in this lesson? Are you an "if-only-er" or a "what if-er" or both? How can you apply the truths of this lesson to your personal needs? What steps will you take to live just one day at a time?

Notes

1. Jay Adams, *From Forgiven to Forgiving* (Amityville, NY: Calvary Press, 1994), 62.

2. Charles Allen, *Victory in the Valleys of Life* (Old Tappan, NJ: Fleming H. Revell Co., 1981), 68.

3. Ken Sande, *The Peacemaker* (Grand Rapids: Baker Books, 2004), 209.

4. Elliot, 162.

5. Elizabeth Cheney.

Count Your Blessings

*"Blessed be the L*ORD*, who daily loadeth us with benefits"*
(Psalm 68:19).

Have you sung the words "Count your many blessings, name them one by one, And it will surprise you what the Lord hath done"? Do you spend more time counting your blessings or naming your complaints? It is so easy to develop a negative attitude that always sees the dark side. However, if we do this, we are going to feel low much of the time because our attitude determines our altitude—how high or how low we feel. The high-altitude attitude allows us to rise above negative thinking.

If we are going to have joy in the midst of our trials, we must develop a positive attitude that allows us to count our blessings. I once read that life is 10 percent what happens to me and 90 percent how I react to it. I must daily choose a positive or negative attitude. I can choose to be a complainer, or I can choose to think positively. Let's learn how to have a positive attitude about life and start counting our blessings.

1. List some of your blessings one by one.

Life, Family, Health, Church, Job, Home, Food, Water, Comforts of Life

2. How would you define "attitude"?

Our way of thinking

James MacDonald says, "Our attitudes are patterns of thinking . . . formed over a long period of time. . . . We get so used to reacting a certain way that our choices become automatic, and in time we cease to see them as actual choices. . . . You can't change an attitude until you admit you chose it. . . . By admitting you made the choice, you put yourself in a position to make a different choice next time."[1]

Negative Thinking

Many people do not count their blessings because they are counting their complaints; e.g., This is bad, and that is bad; she is wrong, and he is wrong. The complainers' days are filled with negative thinking. Negative thinking is one of the biggest robbers of joy, and it is a choice people make.

3. What people in the Bible are remembered as murmurers and complainers? Read Exodus 16:7 and 8; Numbers 14:27; 16:11; 17:5; 1 Corinthians 10:10.

4. Read Numbers 11:1–3. How did God react to the people's murmuring and complaining?

5. Read 1 Corinthians 10:11. Most of the Old Testament is the history of God's people, the Israelites. Why were these details recorded?

Examples for us

6. Can we blame a bad attitude on our parents or other people? Why or why not? *No / We have free will*

7. Why is complaining sin? Read James 4:17 and 1 Thessalonians 5:18.

James MacDonald explains that "unfortunately, there is a kind of low-altitude life that too many people live. . . . It's a down-and-dirty, cloudy, damp, depressing, ungrateful, unthankful, complaining, negative, ugh! sort of living. . . . But there is another kind of living. It's a high-altitude attitude. . . . This life soars above and refuses to focus on the negative. If you have ever flown up there, then you know that's where we want to live our lives."[2]

Positive Thinking

8. "Your attitude determines your altitude." What does that statement mean to you?

9. Respond to this statement: "Life is 10 percent what happens to me and 90 percent how I react to it."

10. If life is 90 percent how we react to it, why is it imperative to keep a positive attitude? Read Philippians 4:13.

11. God's Word tells us to "offer the sacrifice of praise to God continually" (Hebrews 13:15). What are some negative attitudes and feelings we might have to "sacrifice," or turn loose, in order to offer praise to God in every circumstance of life?

Resentment, Jealousy

"Change your attitude," writes Donald Morgan. "Get it into high gear. Make it positive and constructive. When you do that, you take the initiative. You take charge. You get the best in yourself and the best beyond yourself going for you. . . . Your attitude determines how you see things, and how you see things determines what you can do about them."[3]

12. First Thessalonians 5:18 says, "In every thing give thanks." What can we be thankful for in the midst of our trials? Read 1 Corinthians 10:13.

No matter how bad our circumstances, we can choose and change our attitude. Donald Morgan tells about Dr. Viktor Frankl, a famous Viennese psychoanalyst. "Many of his greatest insights came out of World War II experiences, when he was in a concentration camp. He was deprived of everything that makes for human decency. . . . But Frankl saw there was one thing his Nazi captors couldn't take from him: his freedom to decide how he would react. 'Love your enemies,' said Jesus (Matthew 5:44). . . Love is the greatest power on earth. . . . So long as you love, you retain mastery over the situation."[4]

13. The last part of 1 Thessalonians 5:18 says, "For this is the will of God in Christ Jesus concerning you." Why does complaining actually question God's sovereignty?

14. Read Psalm 68:19. What is another way to have a positive attitude rather than a complaining one?

15. Read Romans 5:3–5 and James 1:2–4. For what can we be thankful in the midst of trials? *We will develop patience + grow in the Lord*

16. Think of a recent trial. As hard as it may have been, for what can you be thankful?

Matthew Henry, a well-known commentator of the nineteenth century, was once held up by robbers. He wrote this about his experience: "Let me be thankful, first, because I was never robbed before; second, because although they took my purse, they did not take my life; third, because although they took my all, it was not much; and fourth, because it was I who was robbed, not I who robbed!"[5]

Remember our attitude determines our altitude. After studying this lesson, can you see more clearly what kind of life you have been living?

17. Have you been flying high with a positive attitude or flying low with a negative attitude? What needs to change?

18. Do you see the blessings of a positive attitude in your life? If so, what are some of them?

Makes everyone happier

FROM MY HEART

Are there people you do not look forward to being around? Why? Is it because they are always negative, always complaining? It doesn't take too long for a negative attitude like that to affect my attitude. An unthankful, complaining attitude is infectious; it contaminates everything around it. I want to get away from that kind of person.

"What if I live with that kind of person?" you may ask. Work hard to find something positive about which you can be thankful each day— beyond the person you live with. Your positive attitude can affect the other person's negative attitude just as much as a negative attitude affects you.

Have you read the story of Pollyana, the little orphan who was sent to live with a cantankerous aunt who didn't want her? The attitude in her aunt's home and the whole town began to be transformed when Pollyanna taught the joyless, thankless town the "The Glad Game." At first, people made fun of Pollyanna when she insisted on finding something to be glad about every time anything bad happened. But ultimately the people were changed by her positive attitude.

Our lives can change when we begin counting our blessings each day, instead of counting our complaints. We can have joy in the midst of our trials if we choose a positive attitude.

I wish there were some wonderful place
In the Land of Beginning Again;
Where all our mistakes and all our heartaches
And all of our poor selfish grief
Could be dropped like a shabby old coat at the door,
And never put on again.[6]

There is a land of beginning again, and it is here and now. God calls it being born again (John 3:3). When we are born again, old things pass away and all things become new (2 Corinthians 5:17). If you have not been born again, I urge you to make this decision today. Read the Scripture verses on pages 5 and 6. When you are born again, God's Holy Spirit lives within you, giving you the power you need to obey God's commands. This is supernatural power, the power that raised Jesus from the dead (Ephesians 3:16). With the help of the Holy Spirit, we can say with Paul, "I can do all things through Christ which strengtheneth me" (Philippians 4:13).

FROM YOUR HEART

If you make the decision to receive God's gift of eternal life and be born again, I would love to hear from you at the address below. Also be sure to share your decision with your Bible study leader.

If you already are a believer, do you need to make any changes in your life after learning how destructive a complaining attitude can be? What impressed you the most about the value of a thankful attitude? How can you help yourself or someone else apply what you have learned?

Juanita Purcell
c/o Regular Baptist Press
1300 North Meacham Road
Schaumburg, Illinois 60173

Notes

1. James MacDonald, 31, 32.

2. Ibid., 58.

3. Donald W. Morgan, *How to Get It Together When Your World Is Coming Apart* (Grand Rapids: Baker Books, 1988), 176, 177.

4. Ibid., 177, 178.

5. DeMoss, 15, 16.

6. Louise Tarkington, quoted by Morgan, 179.

LEADER'S
GUIDE

Suggestions for Leaders

The Bible is a living and powerful book! It is God speaking to us today. Every opportunity to learn from it is a precious privilege. As you use this study guide, be flexible. It is simply a tool to aid in the understanding of God's Word. Adapt it to suit your unique group of women and their needs. Use the questions as you see fit; the answers are provided to clarify my intent and stimulate your thoughts. You may have an entirely different insight as the Holy Spirit illumines your heart and mind.

The effectiveness of a group Bible study usually depends on two things: the leader herself and the ladies' commitment to prepare beforehand and to interact during the study. You cannot totally control the second factor, but you have total control over the first one. These brief suggestions will help you be an effective Bible study leader.

You will want to prepare each lesson a week in advance. During the week, read supplemental material and look for illustrations in the everyday events of your life as well as in the lives of others.

Encourage the ladies in the Bible study to complete each lesson before the meeting itself. This preparation will make the discussion more interesting. You can suggest that ladies answer two or three questions a day as part of their daily Bible reading time rather than trying to do the entire lesson at one sitting.

You may also want to encourage the ladies to memorize the key verse for each lesson. (This is the verse that is printed in italics at the start of each lesson.) If possible, print the verses on 3" x 5" cards to distribute each week. If you cannot do this, suggest that the ladies make their own cards and keep them in a prominent place throughout the week.

The physical setting in which you meet will have some bearing on the study itself. An informal circle of chairs, chairs around a table, someone's living room or family room—these types of settings encourage people to relax and participate. In addition to an informal setting, create an atmosphere in which ladies feel free to participate and be themselves.

You can plan your own format or adapt this one to meet your needs.

1 ½-hour Bible Study

10:00—10:30 Bible study

Leader guides discussion of half the questions in the day's lesson.

10:30—10:45 Coffee and fellowship

10:45—11:15 Bible study

Leader continues discussion of the questions in the day's lesson.

11:15—11:30 Prayer time

Answers for Leader's Use

Information inside parentheses ( ) is instruction for the group leader.

LESSON 1

1. Man is born to trouble; it can be expected.

2. *Matthew 5:11*—People will insult us, persecute us, and tell lies about us. *John 15:20*—Christ's followers will be persecuted just as He was. *Romans 8:17*—To share in His glory, we will share in His suffering. (Discuss what He suffered that we might also have to suffer.) *2 Timothy 3:12*—Every Christian who wants to live a godly life will be persecuted. (Discuss: We may not face prison or starvation, but what kinds of persecution may we face?) *James 1:2, 3*—Trials are to be expected. *1 Peter 2:21*—Christ's suffering was an example that we will suffer also.

3. (a) "And we know." (b) Trials are part of the "all things" God is going to use for our spiritual good to make us more like Christ.

4. When we start dwelling on our problems too much, we can forget all of the precious promises we have learned from God's Word. We can begin to doubt God's love and faithfulness to us.

5. *Psalm 34:8*—God is good, no matter what happens. *Psalm 145:17*—God is righteous and holy, and all He does is righteous and holy. *Jeremiah 31:3*—God's love is everlasting, unfailing, and unconditional. (Human love is often conditional: you love me, I'll love you.) *2 Thessalonians 1:5, 6*—God's judgments are always right. *Hebrews 13:5, 6*—God is always with us.

6. Keep trusting God and keep relying upon His Word. We know that what God is doing is for our spiritual good—even if we don't understand the process.

7. Bring them into captivity to the obedience of Christ.

8. We must replace our negative thoughts with the truths of God's Word.

9. When God starts a project, He will complete it. When you get discouraged, remember that God won't give up on you. He has promised to complete the work He started in you when He saved you.

10. We grow more through adversity than through easy roads and flower-strewn paths. Adversity is an effective way for God to get our attention.

11. Spiritual good. The ultimate good God has in mind for us is to become like His Son, Jesus Christ.

12. To those who love God and who are called according to His purpose.

13. She obeys God's Word.

14. God had a purpose in mind when He saved us. Verse 29 explains the purpose—to be like Jesus.

15. *1 Peter 1:6, 7*—Trials prove that our faith is genuine, and this, in turn, brings praise and honor to God. *Psalm 119:71*—Affliction is good for us because it draws us to God's Word. *2 Corinthians 12:7–10*—Trials help us find our strength in God alone and thus bring glory to Him.

16. When we are hurting and no one can help us, we realize we need God's supernatural strength. This realization forces us to lean upon Christ for His strength.

17. (Begin the discussion by sharing what is happening in your life. Encourage the ladies to share their experiences.)

LESSON 2

1. *1 Chronicles 29:11, 12*—God is in control; He is exalted above all and can do as He chooses. *Psalm 115:3*—God does whatever He pleases. *Isaiah 46:9, 10*—God knows the end of everything; He will do as He pleases to fulfill His plan. *Daniel 4:17, 34, 35*—God, the Most High, rules over the kingdoms of men. No one can question Him. *Ecclesiastes 7:14*—God has appointed both prosperity and adversity.

2. (a) To honor or praise the person. (b) To honor God before other people. We make God "visible" as we reflect His likeness to others.

3. (Ask a few ladies to share their experience or the testimony of someone else.)

4. "That the works of God should be made manifest in him." In other words, to make God visible to others.

5. Jesus made clay with His spit and put it on the man's eyes. He then told the man to wash in the pool of Siloam.

6. (Ask one or two ladies to share their experiences.)

7. To make Paul fully dependent on Christ's power; thus God was glorified, not Paul.

8. He gloried in his trial because it was an opportunity to make God's power visible in his life.

9. God's grace was sufficient for his every need. When Paul was weak and helpless, he became strong through God's power.

10. Whatever Paul accomplished was due to God's power; thus God was glorified, not Paul.

11. (a) By believing God's promise through faith. (b) To give him a son in his old age. (c) It appears God wanted to stretch Abraham's faith. He waited until all of Abraham's natural strength to bear a son was gone. Could it be that it was Abraham's faith that gave him strength to bring forth a son in his old age?

12. He fell down at Christ's feet and thanked Him for showing mercy to him and healing him.

13. Giving testimony is commanded; it is an encouragement to others; it is a way to acknowledge God's work in our lives. (If you have time, encourage several ladies

to give public testimony to God's work in their lives in a difficult time.)

14. Their strength is small. They try to make it in their own strength instead of Christ's strength working through them.

15. Spend time with the Lord each day; wait on Him; exchange our weak strength for His supernatural strength.

16. Job glorified God by not turning against Him even when everything possible had gone wrong in his life. Job is an example to us of the strength God can give a person in the midst of suffering.

17. God can do anything; His plans will be accomplished.

18. Her songs focus on God and His wonderful works. These songs have enriched and encouraged thousands of God's people through the years.

LESSON 3

1. They correct with words and the rod of correction (spanking).

2. He chastens us. "Chastening" is the same word for "correction," or "discipline."

3. The Lord disciplines those whom He loves.

4. They don't love them enough to care about their moral and spiritual well-being.

5. God disciplines for our good, or profit, so that our lives will be more holy.

6. God's discipline is not just to make us good but to make us godly. God is always thinking of our spiritual good. We may not see it as good because we are usually thinking about our physical good.

7. "Scourgeth."

8. It can be very severe at times.

9. We need to regularly ask God to convict us of the sin in our lives—even sins of which we may not be aware. Then, if a trial comes and we know there is no known sin in our lives, we know the trial is not chastening or discipline; it is God's way of stretching our faith so we can grow spiritually.

10. The final outcome of sin is death. (Notice the severe punishment for sin in 1 Corinthians 11:29 and 30.) When sin is allowed to go unchecked in our lives, it spreads like a cancer, causing all kinds of problems.

11. Such a person is only a professor—not a possessor—of salvation.

12. Jonah ran away from what he knew God wanted him to do.

13. God sent the storm that eventually landed Jonah in the sea; and God prepared the fish to swallow Jonah. God had Jonah in the right place for His plan to be accomplished.

14. He prayed.

15. Obedience to God's will.

16. Three days and nights.

17. The law of the harvest: If we sow disobedience, we will reap correction. We live with the consequences of our actions.

18. (Share an illustration from your own life, if possible. Then ask one or two volunteers to share a lesson they have learned.)

LESSON 4

1. Both of these verses say "when"—not "if"—regarding trials. Trials will come! We don't know when they will come, but we know they will come because they are part of the process of moving toward spiritual maturity.

2. God's peace.

3. We know they are for our spiritual good to make us more like Jesus.

4. We will become bitter, and this bitterness will affect ourselves and others.

5. Surgery is for our good, even though pain is involved. Some medicines taste bad, but we know they will help us. We endure the pain or bad taste because we know the good outcome of the surgery or medicine.

6. We might stop our Bible reading and prayer; we might not want to fellowship with God's people; we might actually get upset with God for allowing our trials.

7. Happy, or blessed.

8. (Have a few ladies share what they wrote. My version: "We know God sends trials to produce a quality of faith in us that will endure trials and not run from them when they come.")

9. We try to get out from under the trial rather than enduring it.

10. To be blessed, or happy, and receive the crown of life.

11. (a) Perfect, establish, strengthen, settle. (b) Trials cause our faith to mature, to be confirmed, to be stable, and to be grounded. (Other words may also be used.)

12. We start figuring out how we can fix things or people.

13. It is from God and is given liberally; it is pure, peaceable, gentle, reasonable, full of mercy and good works; it is not hypocritical.

14. We are dwelling on our problems and how we can fix them and trying to dwell on God's promises at the same time—we are double-minded. We need to keep our eyes fixed on God's promises rather than on how we can fix our problems.

15. We must stop leaning on our own understanding and start trusting God, acknowledging that His ways are right.

16. The Bible says, "Let him ask." Furthermore, God does not begrudge having to help us ("upbraideth not").

17. (Ask a few ladies to share their thoughts.)

18. Trials develop endurance. Therefore, when trials come, we don't run from them; we learn from them. We just keep on doing what needs to be done without quitting—whether we feel like it or not!

LESSON 5

1. *1 Thessalonians 5:18*—Everything that happens to me is part of God's will for me, so I should thank God for it. *Ephesians 5:20*—God wants me to have an attitude of gratitude—no matter what.

2. They are both commands to thank God for everything. We can always be thankful that God is in control and that nothing can touch our lives that He does not allow.

3. (a) We are most likely to say it when things are going well and everything is smooth in our lives. (b) We are least likely to say it when we are experiencing trials and are wondering if God is being merciful and faithful to us.

4. God is good all the time. His compassions fail not; His mercies are new every morning (to meet whatever we face that day); His faithfulness is great.

5. (Have a few ladies share their definitions. The basic idea is the feeling we have when our expectations are not met.)

6. God orders our steps. When God brings about circumstances to stop us or detour us in our plans, we often experience disappointment until we realize God has a plan for us.

7. God knows about our lives and has planned an "expected end," a future full of hope.

8. Discouragement.

9. (Let several ladies share their definitions. The idea is "lack of courage or conviction.")

10. They did not believe the report of the two good spies; instead they listened to the ten spies who thought the land could not be taken. They did not believe that God would go before them and fight for them.

11. We must use the Word of God to defeat the discouraging thoughts Satan plants in our minds. We must be alert to Satan's tricks and schemes to defeat us. We must learn to capture our thoughts, or Satan will take us captive with his thoughts.

12. Being unthankful or ungrateful.

13. Only one out of the ten healed lepers thanked God for His healing. People take God's blessings for granted.

14. Through the supernatural power that is available to us through Christ. This supernatural power in us is the same power that raised Christ from the dead.

15. Giving thanks is an act of the will—not an emotional response. If we don't obey the command—regardless of our feelings—we sin.

16. (Compile a list from the ladies' answers.)

17. (a) Thankfulness is a choice or an act of obedience. (b) God's wonderful works.

18. (Ask volunteers to share their answers.)

19. (Share something from your own life, if possible; then ask one or two volunteers to share.)

LESSON 6

1. (a) Hands open, palms up. (b) My description of palms-up living is releasing my grip on everything and every person in my life; it is putting my palms up and saying, "Lord, it all belongs to You; give what You want and take what You want."

2. It can help you have a spirit of acceptance, rather than resisting and resenting what God is allowing.

3. We have the power of the Holy Spirit working in us to help us. This is the same power that raised Christ from the dead; it is supernatural power.

4. Deny self; take up the cross; follow Jesus.

5. Our bodies; that is, ourselves.

6. We are living sacrifices.

7. Christ offered His body as a sacrifice in complete surrender to the will of God to pay for our sins and to reconcile us to Himself. It is a reasonable thing for us to offer our bodies to Him as living sacrifices.

8. Everything.

9. Our love for Christ must come before our love for our families or even our own lives.

10. An overnight stay in a den of lions.

11. God sent his angel to shut the lions' mouths, and Daniel was not hurt.

12. They were cast into a fiery furnace.

13. They were not burned by the fire. The Angel of the Lord delivered them.

14. They showed an attitude of total acceptance of God's will by determining to obey God regardless of what the consequences would be.

15. "Be it unto me according to thy word" (v. 38).

16. It probably cost her the esteem of friends and townspeople; it could have cost her her espousal to Joseph.

17. (Allow a few ladies to share.)

18. The reward will be to hear the Savior say, "Well done, good and faithful servant."

LESSON 7

1. Fortify our lives with the Word of God before the storm comes. Then we will have a shelter to keep us from sinking during the storm.

2. (Ask several volunteers to share their lists.)

3. God wants to guide our lives step-by-step and day by day. He goes before us; we follow Him.

4. (a) God gives us power to rise above our circumstances and to see the big

picture. (b) By waiting on the Lord. (c) Spend time with the Lord, reading and meditating on His Word. Spend time in prayer, letting God speak to us.

5. It keeps us from sinning foolishly by resenting what God is doing or by taking matters into our own hands.

6. *Jeremiah 31:3*—He loves us unconditionally. *Philippians 4:19*—He has promised to supply all our needs. *Isaiah 26:3*—He promises peace if we will trust Him. *Hebrews 13:5*—He will never leave us. *Hebrews 13:6*—He will help us.

7. Don't worry about anything; pray about everything; thank the Lord for everything.

8. He was in prison, facing the possibility of death.

9. Contentment does not come to us as a gift when we are born again. It is something we learn as we grow in our relationship with Christ and apply His promises to our daily lives.

10. (a) Our own strength leads to defeat; God's strength leads to victory. (b) We must daily say no to the "old man" (our way of life before we were born again) and yes to the Holy Spirit, Who wants to have control of our lives (Gal. 5:16). It is a daily putting off and a daily putting on.

11. (a) It may be because we get our needs and our wants mixed up. (b) Ask one or two ladies to share their experiences.)

12. (a) Satan. Adam was afraid after he sinned (Gen. 3:10). (b) Fear is torment; it displaces love in our lives.

13. (a) Times of severe testing. (b) We will make it through the trial.

14. We are dwelling on something that is positive (God's promises), not on our problems (negative). I start going over my "Why Sink When You Can Swim?" verses, and soon my anxiety is replaced with God's peace.

15. We are trusting our feelings, not God's Word. God never moves; He is always with us. See Psalm 139:7–12.

16. God knows what He is doing. He knows what is going on in my life. His hand is controlling the thermostat of the fiery furnace, and He knows when to turn down the heat.

17. Our love is often conditional—you love me, I'll love you. Unconditional love says, "I'll love you no matter what you do."

18. (Ask two or three ladies to share their verses. Here is my version: "God's way is always perfect. His Word has proven that to me. I am safe and secure when I trust Him completely.")

19. God is not a shifting shadow; He is always the same.

LESSON 8

1. Elijah and the prophets of Baal each would build an altar and prepare a sacrifice, but they would light no fire. The G(g)od Who sent fire would be the true God.

2. The prophets of Baal called on their god, but to no avail; no answer ever came. Elijah soaked his altar and sacrifice with water; then he called on the Lord. God sent fire that consumed the sacrifice, the wood, the stones, and all the water.

3. He promised rest in the midst of the burdens and trials.

4. We keep rehearsing our hurts, and that keeps the wounds open and we can't heal. We must start rehearsing God's promises; they bring healing and rest.

5. Discouragement and self-pity begin to consume us. Remember, we can't feel discouraged unless we are thinking discouraging thoughts.

6. Despair and depression, even thoughts of suicide. Depression is often called a dark pit or tunnel.

7. When our whole world seems to be falling apart, and it doesn't seem things will ever change.

8. The psalmist came to realize that the best course in times of trials is not to run away from the trials but to cast them on the Lord, Who would keep him steady through the trial.

9. (a) When our trial is over, we will come forth as gold. (b) At this point, we are trying to just survive the trial rather than thinking about the outcome.

10. The mind relives and rehearses the pleasant past and the current painful present circumstances. It hurts to think this way, but it seems the person can't think of anything else.

11. The mind becomes so filled with painful problems that the person can no longer think of others or even her own obligations. She is so exhausted from lack of sleep and emotional stress that she doesn't feel like going anywhere. She loses interest in what is happening in the world. She is interested only in her problem.

12. The person needs to get her mind off herself and her problem and fix her mind on Christ. She needs to dwell on God's promises instead of her problems. The solution is to replace dwelling on problems with dwelling on promises.

13. "Hope thou in God: for I shall yet praise him." The psalmist had not lost his hope in God. People in depression have lost hope that God will ever help them, lost hope that people will understand them, and lost hope that their circumstances will ever change.

14. Only God could put a smile on his face again.

15. Sleeplessness, loss of appetite, diarrhea, headaches, fatigue, rapid heartbeat—and many more.

16. Thyroid problems, lack of estrogen, and recovery from stroke or heart attack are some physical causes for depression. Check with your doctor if you suspect symptoms of these problems or if you experience other physical problems that could cause depression.

17. Focus our minds on Christ and trust Him to meet our needs. (I can't emphasize enough that we need to rehearse God's promises rather than our problems.)

18. (Ask two or three ladies to share how they have been helped.)

LESSON 9

1. God is our refuge and strength; He is a constant help in time of trouble.

2. Be still and recognize Him as God. (The Hebrew word translated "be still" literally means "be relaxed—take your hands off." Palms-up living can be a great help in obeying this command.)

3. As a mother comforts her children.

4. "Everlasting consolation." He will console and comfort us forever.

5. Jesus Christ experienced everything we will ever experience. He knows how we feel when we suffer and feel so alone. Someone may say, "If God loved me, He wouldn't let me suffer like this." Did God the Father love His Son when He was suffering on the cross? Yes! Christ had to suffer and feel forsaken to know how we feel and to be able to empathize with us.

6. Jesus knows how we feel! He became flesh and blood so He could know the human experience and deliver us from our fears.

7. He comforts us in the same way Jesus does. He abides within us. (The word translated "Comforter" is from the Greek word that means "one called alongside to help." The same word is used in 1 John 2:1, where Jesus is called our "advocate.")

8. He strengthens our inner person with His might. (The Holy Spirit is God; He is omnipotent!)

9. Gives us hope.

10. Understanding; a listening ear.

11. Verbalizing helps us work through our feelings.

12. Full of reproach and heaviness; tearful.

13. Someone who has had similar heartaches and trials and has experienced God's comfort.

14. *David*—cause: his sin of adultery with Bathsheba; resolution: he confessed his sin and was forgiven and restored. *Naomi*—cause: the move to Moab and the death of her sons and husband; resolution: her return to Bethlehem; her daughter-in-law's marriage to Boaz and the birth of their child. *Joseph*—cause: mistreatment at the hand of his brothers (and later by his master, Potiphar); resolution: he was able to see that what man meant for evil, God meant for good. *Mary and Martha*—cause: the death of their brother; resolution: the miracle of resurrection. (Other Biblical characters to consider are Peter [his sin of denial and Jesus' restoration of him for service]; Hagar [her mistreatment at the hand of her mistress and then God's provision of water and His promise that her son would also be great; Gen. 21].)

15. To "sympathize" is to feel sorrow for someone. To "empathize" is to know how the other person feels because you have had a similar experience.

16. We can share how God has strengthened and encouraged us and what spiritual lessons we learned as a result of our trial.

LESSON 10

1. Joy is a deep sense of trust and peace in the soul.

2. Joy is found in the presence of Christ; that is, our relationship with Him. Someone has observed that happiness depends on happenings and that joy depends upon our relationship with Jesus Christ.

3. (a) The fig tree doesn't blossom; no fruit is on the vines; the olives don't produce; the fields yield no meat; the flock is cut off; there's no herd in the stalls. (b) "Yet"—in spite of all those things—"I will rejoice in the LORD."

4. Joy is part of the fruit of the Spirit. He produces it in us as we depend on Him.

5. (These are personal answers. Encourage the ladies to examine their hearts and write down their thoughts.)

6. To keep my eyes on Christ instead of on my circumstances is to dwell on God's promises instead of on my problems.

7. People can forsake us and even become our enemies. Circumstances can become so devastating we feel totally overwhelmed.

8. Our attitude determines our altitude. Only as we keep our eyes on Christ can we keep a positive attitude about life and look up.

9. He began to sink.

10. We will begin to sink under our circumstances instead of staying on top of them if we get our eyes off Christ.

11. The person is double-minded, or unstable—up one day and down the next. What she focuses on determines whether she is up or down.

12. We can err from our faith and experience the same sorrows the world experiences. Money never satisfies; you always want just a little more. The love of money is a downward spiritual spiral.

13. Americans—compared to most of the rest of the world's people—are rich in this world's goods. But joy is not found in material things. Money can buy a home, but not happiness. It can buy luxury, but not contentment.

14. (a) Contentment is being satisfied with what you have. (b) Contentment is something we learn in the midst of life's experiences.

15. Christ's supernatural power.

16. (Ask a volunteer or two to share her answer and why she gave herself that grade.)

17. To maintain one's spiritual life is to keep studying and applying God's Word; to confess sins; to walk in the Spirit. (The ladies may be able to suggest other verses and other facets of maintaining one's spiritual life.)

18. The psalmists emphasized daily prayer, meditation, and praise. We can't live on yesterday's spiritual feeding anymore than we can live on yesterday's physical feeding. We need nourishment each day—physically as well as spiritually.

19. (Ask a few ladies to share how they have their daily devotions.)

20. It is as good as medicine.

LESSON 11

1. An "if only-er" says, "If only I had done or had not done this or that." A "what if-er" says, "What if this or that happens?" "If only" focuses on the past and wishes it could be done over; "what if" focuses on the future and wants the circumstances to be different.

2. Destructive guilt is telling yourself how bad you are, even though you may have asked for and received forgiveness. Destructive guilt has no good outcome. Constructive guilt leads to something positive. It is confessing you have broken God's commandments and are in need of forgiveness.

3. Confess sin to God and accept, by faith, the forgiveness that He grants. Do not continue to rehash the sin. Psalm 32:5 says that when we confess, God "forgavest the iniquity of my sin."

4. If the sin has truly been confessed, then God has forgiven. The person must ask God to help her forget the things that are behind. Destructive guilt will hold a person hostage and diminish her joy and her usefulness to God.

5. God has forgiven me and will not bring up my sin again. I need to quit dwelling on it and bringing it up in my mind again. If you are having a hard time dwelling on something constructive, get out your "Why Sink When You Can Swim?" verses and start dwelling on them.

6. Accepting God's forgiveness is healing for the soul and allows us to avoid a pit of despondency. We must acknowledge that God is the only One Who can forgive sin and remove its penalty.

7. It means God will not bring up this sin to us again. Forgetting is passive; we just do it. Not remembering is active—a choice we make. God chooses not to remember. (When we choose not to dwell on an issue or bring it up to someone else or ourselves, we are choosing not to remember.)

8. Satan.

9. We need to forgive because we have been forgiven. (Nothing that is done against us is as great as our sin against God. We have been forgiven much; we need to forgive much.)

10. We cannot do it in our own strength. When we avail ourselves of God's supernatural strength in us, we can do everything God commands us to do. "Renew" in Isaiah 40:31 also means "exchange." We can exchange our weak strength for God's supernatural strength. What an exchange!

11. *Joseph*—His brothers wanted to kill him, but instead sold him to Midianite traders, who took him to Egypt. Joseph chose to forgive his brothers because he realized that what they meant for evil, God used for good. *Stephen*—He preached the truth of the gospel to the Jewish leaders, and they stoned him to death. Before he died, he forgave his persecutors, saying they did not know what they were doing. *Jesus*—He was crucified, but He forgave those who committed the awful act.

12. (Challenge the ladies to be honest. This can be a time whey they free themselves of guilt and an unforgiving spirit.)

13. Normal precaution applies to things such as fire, poison, health care, and things over which we have a measure of control. Fretful worry is dwelling on things over which we have no control and things we cannot change.

14. "I don't believe You." "I don't trust You."

15. Sin.

16. Sleeplessness, ulcers, weight gain or loss, headaches, high blood pressure, many others.

17. (v. 4) Rejoice in the Lord; (v. 5) recognize God's presence; (v. 6) determine to give up being anxious; (v. 6) pray about everything; (v. 6) be thankful; (v. 8) focus our thinking on positive things; (v. 9) do the things we know to be right; (v. 10) think about others; (v. 11) learn to be content; (v. 13) accept Christ's strength; (v. 19) trust God to supply our needs.

18. (List the things the ladies suggest. Ideas include memorizing Philippians 4; writing the truths on individual cards and meditating on them; asking, Which truth from Philippians 4 applies to this worry or concern?)

LESSON 12

1. (Ask the ladies to share their lists.)

2. A pattern of thinking; a way of approaching life.

3. The Israelites.

4. God was angry with them and sent fire to the camp.

5. As an example for us. For instance, we see the effect complaining and murmuring have on us and our families.

6. We cannot blame our bad attitudes on others or our circumstances. To have a negative, complaining attitude is a personal choice. People and circumstances may make it harder to have a good attitude, but we always have plenty of things to be thankful for.

7. I can't complain and be thankful at the same time. So, if I choose complaining, I am not obeying 1 Thessalonians 5:18; disobedience is sin. Knowing to do right (e.g., having a good attitude) and not doing it is sin.

8. (Ask a few ladies to share their thoughts. How high or how low we feel is determined by our attitude.)

9. (Ask volunteers to share their thoughts. My attitude determines my actions and reactions.)

10. If I keep a positive attitude, I know there is nothing that can happen to me that I cannot handle with God's help and strength.

11. Possible answers include anger, bitterness, hatred, revenge, and jealousy.

12. We can be thankful that God in control of the trials and the circumstances surrounding them; He will never give us more than we can bear.

13. Trials come because God either planned them or permitted them. They are His will and are for our good (Rom. 8:28, 29). To complain about trials is to say that God doesn't know what He is doing.

14. If we dwell on all our daily benefits, we will have a positive attitude.

15. God is involved in a process in our lives. He starts with trials and ends with hope (assurance). God is stretching our faith so we can learn to trust Him and not run away from our trials.

16. (Ask two or three volunteers to share their experiences.)

17. (This is a personal reflection question.)

18. (List the blessings the ladies name.)